# ACPL ITEM
3 1833 0141 9 8
# DISCAR

D1555120

*338 C438L
Chinloy, Peter, 1950-
Labor productivity

7038947

*338 C438L
Chinloy, Peter, 1950-
Labor productivity

7553113

## ALLEN COUNTY PUBLIC LIBRARY

## FORT WAYNE, INDIANA 46802

You may return this book to any agency, branch,
or bookmobile of the Allen County Public Library

DEMCO

# LABOR PRODUCTIVITY

# LABOR PRODUCTIVITY

## Peter Chinloy

Abt Books / Cambridge, Massachusetts

ALLEN COUNTY PUBLIC LIBRARY
FORT WAYNE, INDIANA

**Library of Congress Cataloging in Publication Data**

Chinloy, Peter, 1950–
    Labor productivity.

    Bibliography: p.
    Includes index.
    1. Labor productivity—United States.    I. Title.
HC110.L3C48          331.11'8'0973          81-3634
ISBN 0-89011-561-3                          AACR2

© Peter Chinloy, 1981

All rights reserved. No part of this publication
may be reproduced or transmitted in any form
or by any means, electronic or mechanical,
including photocopy, recording, or any
information storage or retrieval system, without
specific permission in writing from the
publisher: Abt Books, 55 Wheeler Street,
Cambridge, MA 02138.

Printed in the United States of America

# CONTENTS

7038947

# LIST OF TABLES

# LIST OF FIGURES

# ACKNOWLEDGMENTS

Several people have made substantial contributions to this research project on the measurement of productivity in the labor market, which has evolved in stages. None of these people shares liability for any of the shortcomings of the work.

Dale Jorgenson provided scholarly guidance at all stages. He encouraged and stimulated my research on the connection between functional forms and index numbers for labor input. In addition, he instilled in me a sense of responsibility and care for the data.

I had as a colleague Frank Gollop. Our work in the area of labor productivity is complementary: his thesis dealt extensively with the industry-by-industry construction of labor input aggregates, while my own research has concentrated on the private domestic economy as the unit of measurement. I am grateful to Gollop and William Barger, who also has performed related research.

Many research assistants in the project provided excellent work in the collection, assembly, computation, and processing of the data. Not all of them can be mentioned here, but I would like to single out some for particular attention. Peter Derksen, an excellent programmer, was responsible for most of the software required to manipulate arrays sometimes containing more than 100,000 cells. Also, invaluable research assistance was provided by David Robinson, Blake Evernden, and Barbara Fraumeni.

There are several others to whom a substantial intellectual debt is owed. Richard Freeman and Robert Hall provided substantial assistance in the formulation of the model. As a scholar, Freeman always stresses the need for robustness in testing and the importance of establishing scholarly lineage. Hall also stressed care in the collection and presentation of the data. Erwin Diewert, my colleague at the University of British Columbia, assisted me in numerous ways. He carefully read several drafts of material contained in this book and made numerous suggestions and comments. I should also mention Charles Blackorby, another colleague, who made constructive comments during the research.

This work on labor productivity has been encouraged by Clark Abt, president of Abt Associates Inc. in Cambridge, Massachusetts. We have had several discussions on areas of mutual interest and have exchanged papers on productivity measurement. In addition, Danny Steinberg and Ernst Stromsdorfer have made several constructive contributions, notably in stressing the study's relevance to public policy and planning purposes.

I am grateful to Abt Books for their editorial aid in the presentation of the work. In particular, Robert Erwin and Nancy Miner are to be thanked for their kindness and assistance. As in many of my other endeavors, an outstanding job in preparing and typing the manuscript has been done by B. Fisher, whose care, diligence, and professionalism have been superb at all times. Also, Susan Dixon was extremely careful in her editing and research on the manuscript.

Finally, I am indebted to my parents, Tom and Almeda Chinloy for their guidance and support over a long period. Also, my wife Diana has had great patience and understanding during the course of the project.

Peter Chinloy
Vancouver, B.C.

# 1

# INTRODUCTION:
# THE PRODUCTIVITY CRISIS
# AND THE LABOR MARKET

Over the period 1900–1960, there has been a long-term increase in productivity, or output per unit of aggregate input, in observed growth performance of Western nations. However, there is no inherent reason for the continuation or perpetuation of long-term productivity increase. If this growth is to be maintained and not to disappear, it is appropriate to examine and determine its sources or causes.

The pioneering work of Solow (1957) yielded an accounting procedure, where output growth is decomposed into weighted averages of input growths and a residual term. This term has been variously referred to as advances to knowledge, technological change, and the measure of our ignorance. While controversy has developed over issues of specification and measurement, the procedure remains the underlying method for explaining growth.

Subsequent issues in productivity growth include such technical considerations as the specification of the underlying form for functions aggregating prices or quantities. It has been shown that relationships exist between functional forms and indices of aggregates. Also, new functional forms have been derived.

For output, the issue is whether value added or gross output should be used. In the former case the explanatory inputs are labor and raw materials. The latter specification also includes the effects of raw materials and fuels. This poses the question of appropriate consideration of produced means of production. Moreover, if capital and energy or fuels are found to be complementary, increases in prices of the latter may prove to be deleterious to productivity growth.

These issues are important in deriving productivity estimates, but the focus of this research is on the labor market. This is a return to earlier productivity questions, which were concerned with explaining output per hour or per employee rather than output per unit of inputs. Indeed, the published series on productivity, despite extensive theoretical developments, continue to be based on output per hour.

An hour worked by a worker with extensive experience, skill, and training will yield a higher output level than an hour worked by one with no such training. This requires an adjustment of hours worked by an efficiency index or labor quality. The underlying objective is to construct estimates of labor quality that appropriately augment the labor services used in production. In turn, labor quality influences productivity change.

Embedded in the definition of labor quality is a description of the work force. In this case, employment is classified by education, occupation, class of worker, age, and sex. These characteristics are viewed as sources of quality change in labor input.

This research examines the contribution of labor input to the growth of output. Further extensions are required to treat labor force participation and hours worked decisions. Also, the various regulations affecting employment have not all been modeled. Some modeling of unemployment insurance and social security has been carried out. In the former case, the modeling does not include state plans or the procedures involved with experience rating. Other regulations on occupational health and safety are included only insofar as costs appear as supplementary to reported wages.

### Measurement of Labor Input

To derive appropriate measures of labor quality for use in productivity analysis, an extensive data base is required. The theoretical justification for the aggregation techniques and data sources used is described in Chapter 2. Labor input is defined as the product of total hours worked and an index of labor quality. The latter is derived through a procedure weighting 1,600 different types of labor.

The growth rate of the weighted hours index is termed labor input. The difference between this growth rate and that of total hours is termed the growth rate in labor quality. The first stage in the procedure is to specify a function that aggregates labor and nonlabor inputs. If the labor inputs are separable from the nonlabor inputs, an aggregate of labor input is obtainable.

The functional form selected for labor input is the translog. It has been shown that this form has as an exact index number the Törnqvist form. This involves calculating an index based on two-period arithmetic mean moving averages of compensation shares.

The data are constructed annually for 1948–1972 for a classification involving sex, age, education, occupation, and class of worker. The empirical results focus on the decomposition of observed growth in labor input in the U.S. private domestic economy for the period. There are four aggregate components, namely, employment, average annual hours worked per person, labor quality per person, and labor quality per hour.

Over the period 1947–1958, employment grew relatively slowly, at 0.37 percent per annum, with annual hours declining by 0.68 percent per year. The major contribution to labor input growth arises from labor quality, the index of education, occupation, age, and class of worker skills for each sex. Quality per person grew at 0.75 percent annually during that period, and quality per hour by 0.44 percent.

The roles of skills per hour and total hours become reversed during the 1958–1972 period. Although labor input grows at 2.05 percent per annum, employment or quantity components account for 1.70 percent, or 86 percent of the total. Part of this contribution arises from a slowing in the decline in hours worked, to 0.19 percent, while employment growth accelerates to 1.87 percent.

The problem for labor input and productivity growth arises in the labor market. Quality per person falls to a growth rate of 0.12 percent per year, and quality per hour to 0.23 percent. On aggregate, the skill contributions made by education, occupation, sex, age, and class of worker have declined considerably.

### Sources of Quality Change

Given the decline in the relative roles of quality change and total hours, Chapter 3 seeks to make an attribution among various sources. Total labor quality, by analogy to the analysis of variance, is composed of various main and interactive effects. It is possible to isolate the effect of education, for example, in measuring labor quality. In turn, once the percentage of total compensation in the economy accruing to labor is known, the contribution of education to productivity growth can be determined.

The theoretical structure involves the specification of a labor aggregate containing various characteristics. By summing in different ways, various subaggregates can be constructed. Suppose there are only two identifying characteristics of labor, education, and sex. By summing over education, a labor input index containing a sex effect is isolated. By summing over sex, a labor input index containing an education effect is determined.

The method used commences with a production function and its associated labor subaggregate. If this subaggregate can be constructed, there is an associated dual wage subaggregate. This starting point yields the same estimates.

The advantage of the proposed procedures is that no estimation of parameters is necessary. Rather, it suffices to calculate the appropriate index number, also specified as Törnqvist. Given that the number of quadratic parameters of second order is $N(N-1)/2$, where $N$ is the number of factors, this is large for 1,600 factors.

Estimates of sources of quality change are presented for the U.S. private domestic economy for the 1947–1974 period. Among the quality change components taken in total, labor quality grows by an average of 0.60 percent per year, accounting for 41 percent of labor input growth. However, for the period 1947–1951 labor quality accounted for 65 percent of total input growth, as compared with only 4.4 percent for 1971–1974.

Among the main effects, declining contributions of education, occupation, and age are dominant. The deteriorating age composition, accounted for by the increasing prevalence of employment among youth, begins in the 1960s and continues through to the mid-1970s. The declining effect of education obtains through to the mid-1970s. Others have chronicled a declining rate of return to education even as relative quantities in total employment increased. The results indicate that the decline in relative wages of the educated has outweighed the increase in relative quantity.

The greatest shift in effect arises in occupational composition. In the 1970s this factor ceases to be a source of growth, turning from a positive contribution of about 0.4 percent annually over the 1967–

1971 period to −0.11 percent for 1971–1974. The major factor making a positive shift is sex composition. Despite the underestimation of discrimination effects, the negative effect of sex composition almost disappears for 1971–1974. If wages are not equal to marginal products, wage differentials as productivity differentials may lead to biases.

The results indicate a deteriorating trend in both educational and occupational composition. The effect of these trends on productivity remains to be determined.

## Labor Skills and Labor Productivity Measurement

Total output involves the contribution of both labor and nonlabor sources. Given the labor quality estimates, Chapter 4 examines the impact on labor productivity and total factor productivity. Growth in output is decomposed into four components in the theoretical structure.

The components are the physical index of nonlabor inputs, a quality index of these inputs, total hours worked, and labor quality. Given that a physical index of nonlabor inputs is difficult to obtain, an efficiency index for all nonlabor inputs is used. The measure of labor productivity used is output per hour worked. The corresponding estimate for total factor productivity is output per unit of an index of inputs.

A relation that relates the two is derived. Specifically, labor productivity growth is expressed as the sum of three components in competitive equilibrium. The three are total factor productivity, the growth of labor quality weighted by the share of labor, and the growth of capital intensity weighted by the share of capital. This provides an accounting for growth in labor productivity.

This relation is examined empirically for the U.S. private domestic economy for the 1947–1974 period. Labor productivity over the whole period averages a 2.61 percent growth rate, but there is a declining trend in this performance. Over 1947–1951 labor productivity grows at 3.66 percent, but this growth rate declines to 0.65 percent in 1971–1974. One of the principal factors causing or associated with the decline is the disappearance of total factor productivity change. The growth rate maintains its historical pattern at about 1 percent per year up to the mid 1960s, at which time a deterioration sets in. The growth rate of total factor productivity is 0.23 percent over 1967–1971 and becomes negative at −0.13 percent for 1971–1974.

Labor quality also contributes to the decline in labor productivity. The labor quality effect is the product of the share of labor in factor compensation and the growth of the quality index. The growth rate of this effect is 0.72 percent annually for 1947–1951, or 19.7 percent of the total. Over 1971–1974 this effect practically disappears, averaging only 0.08 percent per year, or 11.5 percent of the total. In the 1970s there is virtually no growth in either total factor productivity or labor quality.

The final component is capital intensity, or efficiency units of capital used per hour worked. There is also a decline in this effect, defined as capital intensity multiplied by the capital share. This effect decreases from a 1.99 percent annual growth rate for 1947–1951 to 0.70 percent for 1971–1974. Labor productivity increases will accompany efforts to increase capital intensity.

## Aggregation of Inputs and Technical Change

There are various methods by which productive inputs may be aggregated. Three possibilities are suggested in a theoretical structure that is also applicable to the specification of technological change. The first is to group inputs along capital and labor lines, a functional approach established in economic analysis. Another option is to divide inputs into production and nonproduction categories. Specifically, production inputs include equipment and blue-collar labor, while nonproduction inputs include plant and white-collar labor. The third possibility is to group a listing of skilled equipment and skilled labor on the one hand, with unskilled labor and plant on the other.

Technological change is correspondingly examined, to determine whether there is a shift in the production function or augmentation of individual inputs or both. Estimates that support the production-non-production grouping are presented for the U.S. private sector 1947–1972. An associated product of the research is a set of elasticity of substitution estimates in a four–factor classification including equipment, plant, blue-collar labor, and white-collar labor. Imposing the production-nonproduction grouping, the results indicate that plant and white-collar workers are complements and that equipment and blue-collar workers similarly are complements. The remaining components are highly substitutable. Of policy interest is the effect of an investment tax credit, which reduces the user cost of equipment and increases the demand for blue-collar labor.

Technological change is examined in more detail. A series of tests is applied, which indicates that Hicks neutral technical change cannot be rejected by the data.

### Human Capital and Vintage Effects

The supply side of human capital, or training acquisition decisions has been extensively discussed. Individuals weigh returns from a variety of training options and invest in that yielding the highest rate of return. The demand side has been less considered, largely because of an absence of data on age and education of employed persons, appropriately associated with series from the national accounts on nonlabor inputs. Given the existence of such data, as described in this chapter, it is possible to measure these demand effects.

The specification is to group workers into three age categories—younger (16–24), middle-aged (25–64), and older (than 65). Capital services constitute a fourth category. Also, there are separate augmentation factors for each age group. Elasticities of substitution are estimated for all factors in the classification. Capital is found to be aggregable with middle-aged workers. In general, workers of different ages are substitutable, but the estimates of the partial elasticities are in the neighborhood of unity, generally lower than other estimates obtained. The conclusion is that the demand for labor is not perfectly elastic.

### Concluding Remarks

The results indicate continuing problems with the productivity performance of the U.S. private sector. The results depend on various assumptions of the model. Factors are assumed to be paid their marginal products, so the influence of discrimination or monopolistic forces is discounted. Also, the biproportional algorithm imparts an inflexibility in the allocation of labor.

Nevertheless, further research into the performance of labor productivity is required. A structure is detailed and presented here for application to other industries or firms. The sources of growth relation also has a dual based on wage structures. Ultimately, there is a hedonic equation for labor input based upon various characteristics, which provides an understanding of the productivity relation in the labor market.

# 2

# THE MEASUREMENT
# OF LABOR INPUT

Labor input is defined in growth accounting as total hours in efficiency units. The efficiency adjustment corrects for the changing composition of total hours worked.[1] Since total hours worked represents the product of employment and mean hours worked per person, separate efficiency adjustments can be performed for each component. An augmentation of total hours implies diminution of identical magnitude in the wage per hour. A portion of observed wage changes can consequently be attributed to changes in the composition of total hours worked.

The Törnqvist index form is used to aggregate the components of labor input.[2] Separate indices for employment and mean hours worked are constructed. From these indices, observed annual growth in labor input is decomposed into sources associated with total employment, mean annual hours, labor input or quality per person engaged, and quality per hour. This growth accounting structure is applied to the U.S. private domestic economy. Procedures required to construct cross-classifications of employment are developed, including a version of the biproportional algorithm permitting the use of an unlimited number of marginal constraint arrays. Such procedures are applied to the construction of employment and total hours classifications. In addition, reconciliations of household and establishment survey counts are performed. The wage series associated with each cell measures the user cost of labor for that cohort. Distributions are fitted to the published frequency data on wages and salaries.

Employer contributions to supplementary benefits, notably social security, are simulated on the basis of the statutory provisions each year. The resulting series for employment and hours and the sources of labor input growth are subsequently presented.

### Labor Input Aggregation

An aggregate measure of labor input is constructed using the Divisia indexing procedure.[3] Total labor compensation $C(t)$ is defined by

$$C(t) = W(t) L(t) = \sum_{i=1}^{n} W_i(t) L_i(t) \tag{2.1}$$

where $W(t)$ and $L(t)$ denote respectively the wage per hour and the input of aggregate labor at time $t$.[4] There are n constituent components or characteristics of the aggregate, with the wage per hour and labor input of the ith category denoted respectively by $W_i(t)$ and $L_i(t)$.

Separate indices of labor input and wages can be derived from the growth accounting form of (2.1). The Divisia index of labor input is

$$L(t) = \exp \sum_{i=1}^{n} \int_0^t v_i \frac{\dot{L}_i(t)}{L_i(t)} \, dt \tag{2.2}$$

with base value $L(0) = 1$, and $V_i(t) = \dfrac{W_i(t) L_i(t)}{\sum_{i=1}^{n} W_i(t) L_i(t)}$

denoting the relative share in total compensation of the $i$th input. A wage index can be constructed analogously, or it can be derived from the first equality of (2.1). For a discrete data set, the index (2.2) can be approximated

$$L_t = \prod_{i=1}^{n} \prod_{s=1}^{t} \frac{L_{i,s}}{L_{i,s-1}} \overline{V}_{i,s-1} \tag{2.3}$$

as a geometric form of weighting cell relatives with $L_0 = 1$. The weighting term $\overline{V}_{i,s} = (V_{i,s} + V_{i,s-1})/2$ is an arithmetic moving average of observed shares.[5]

Total hours worked in a given period for each cohort represents the product of employment and mean hours worked. Consequently, (2.3) can be expressed as the product of an employment index

$$N_t = \prod_{i-1}^{n} \prod_{s-1}^{t} \frac{N_{i,s}}{N_{i,s-1}} \overline{V}_{i,s} \tag{2.4}$$

and an hours index

$$H_t = \prod_{i-1}^{n} \prod_{s-1}^{t} \frac{H_{i,s}}{H_{i,s-1}} \overline{V}_{i,s} \tag{2.5}$$

in this arithmetic share of Törnqvist form, using the terminology of Diewert (1976, 1980). The index value of employment in year t is represented by $N_t$, and $N_{i,s}$ denotes the number of persons engaged in category $i$ in year $s$, while $H_t$ and $H_{i,s}$ denote respectively the index value of mean hours and the mean hours worked per person in category $i$ in year $s$, and $N_0 = H_0 = 1$.

Separate indices of labor quality for persons engaged and of mean hours are obtained from the ratio of the weighted Törnqvist index to an index unweighted by shares. Hence

$$Q_t^N = \frac{N_t}{N_t^1} \tag{2.6}$$

with

$$Q_t^H = \frac{H_t}{H_t^1} \tag{2.7}$$

and

$$N_t^1 = \prod_{s-1}^{t} \frac{N_{.,s}}{N_{.,s-1}} \tag{2.8}$$

with

$$H_t^1 = \prod_{s-1}^{t} \frac{H_{.,s}}{H_{.,s-1}} \tag{2.9}$$

where $Q_t^N$ and $Q_t^H$ denote respectively quality indices of employment and mean hours, and $N_t^1$ and $H_t^1$ are unweighted indices of these aggregates. In addition, $N_{.,s} = \Sigma_{i-1}^{n} N_{i,s}$ and $H_{.,s} = \Sigma_{i-1}^{n} N_{i,s} H_{i,s}/N_{i,s}$ denote respectively total employment and mean hours worked per person in year $s$. The indices (2.6) through (2.9) are normalized at unity at time zero.

## Employment

There are two economic counts of employment from survey data. A household survey, or count of persons, is based on responses by all employed persons in a given sample of household units. Such a survey yields data on personal characteristics of employed persons in addition to information on earnings and hours worked. The definition of an employed person in the private sector includes private wage and salary employees, self-employed persons, and unpaid family workers. For the U.S., household-based data are derived from a sample in the *Current Population Survey (CPS)* and the decennial census.

An alternative source of employment data is based on an establishment survey, which yields a count of total jobs filled within the private sector. From social security and payroll records, a sample of employers is used to construct the series. The difference between jobs filled in production and jobs held by full-time and part-time employees is the number of self-employed jobs. For establishment data, the jobs terminology is used in place of persons, since no accounting is performed for individual employed persons, and multiple job holders are consequently counted as establishment-based persons engaged by each of their employers.[6] The principal source for establishment-based data is the *National Income and Product Accounts (NIPA)*, published by the Bureau of Economic Analysis (BEA) of the Department of Commerce. This series is derived from a Bureau of Labor Statistics (BLS) employer survey, which yields a count of total jobs in each industry.

Given the existence of household and establishment employment data as alternative measures of persons engaged, the first issue in the construction of an employment measure is the reconciliation of the counts. There are several differences between such series. Unpaid family workers—that is, immediate family members providing labor services in establishments—are not listed as payroll employees or as employed persons. These persons are counted as employed by the household survey, implying that a reconciliation to the household base requires the addition of this total to the establishment count.

A second difference in the two control totals arises from the treatment of multiple job holders. A multiple job holder is defined as a person employed at more than one job within the private sector, being an employee in at least one.[7] Self-employed persons reporting more than one job, all in an entrepreneurial capacity, are excluded. Also excluded are all individuals reporting two jobs of which one is as an unpaid family worker. Private household workers reporting more than one employer are excluded, as are persons holding more than one job, none of which is in the private sector. Finally, government employees holding at least one job in the private sector are counted as private sector multiple job holders. Multiple job holders are counted at each job held, and are consequently counted more than once in the establishment survey and once in the household survey. A reconciliation to the household base therefore requires the subtraction from the establishment count of all secondary jobs held in the private sector by multiple job holders.[8]

An additional reconciling item between the person count and the job count is the treatment of unpaid absentees. Individuals absent without pay are included in the household count but excluded from the establishment count.

The procedure for reconciling establishment vs. household persons engaged is summarized in Figure 2.1. The sum of full- and part-time wage and salary jobs and of full-time proprietor jobs provides an establishment control total within each industry of the private sector.[9] From each control total, a household estimate of engaged persons 14–15 years old is subtracted. Secondary jobs of private multiple job holders are subtracted to yield an adjusted total of employment in contrast to jobs filled, equivalent to a CPS figure but excluding unpaid categories. The household unpaid family worker total is added to the adjusted establishment base figure, to yield total persons at work.[10] These control totals constitute the control industry-specific data for the measurement of labor input. Persons at work are defined as all individuals actively employed in production at the given survey date. The remaining reconciling items are unpaid absentees and an unaccounted discrepancy, which are added to yield the household count of employment.[11] The persons at work total provides an appropriate base for the economic measurement of labor input, since it includes all persons supplying labor services in private production. Given the procedure for reconciling establishment and household series, a linkage of the two counts can be constructed to develop any intermediate definition of employment and to ensure consistency between the two sources.

**Figure 2.1**   Reconciliation of Establishment and Household Employment Series

|  | Full- and part-time wage and salary jobs, and full-time proprietary jobs (BLS = *NIPA*) | (establishment control total) |
|---|---|---|
| LESS: | Secondary jobs held in the private sector by multiple job holders and household employment of persons aged 14–15 | |
| = | Adjusted wage and salary employees and full-time proprietors | |
| ADD: | Unpaid family workers | |
| = | Persons at work | |
| ADD: | Unpaid absentees<br>Unaccounted discrepancy | |
| = | Persons engaged (*CPS*) | (household control total) |

A second issue in the measurement of employment is the economic base covered. For the data base constructed here, the establishment definition for the U.S. private domestic economy excludes all jobs filled in federal, state, and local public administration, government enterprises, and work relief programs. Multiple job holders with primary employment in the government are included if their secondary employment is in a private sector job. The employed persons base total is identical to that reported in the *NIPA*, except that employees in public education are included in the total. The household series is the estimate of annual employment from the *CPS*. The definition of employment includes all full-time and part-time workers in the civilian noninstitutional U.S. population active in the private domestic economy.[12]

The reconciliation of household and establishment data and the definition of employment are two issues not specific to the period covered here. Two issues that are specific to the 1947–1972 period are the accession to statehood of Alaska and Hawaii in 1959 and the survey redefinitions introduced in 1966 for the household series. The effect of the accession of Alaska and Hawaii is chain-linked by the construction of two employment totals for 1960, one including and the other excluding these states.[13] In both the household and establishment surveys, the published data pertain to the former definition.

In 1967 the coverage of the *CPS* household survey increased and revisions were effected in the questionnaire. Survey coverage was increased from 35,000 households in 357 survey areas to 50,000 households in 449 areas.[14] The principal redefinitions are coverage of persons employed aged 16 and over, as opposed to 14 and over, and a reclassification as employees of all persons working in proprietary corporations. The establishment survey covers all persons aged 14 and over. A reconciliation is carried out by subtracting household estimates of 14 and 15 year olds from the establishment-based control total. The establishment and household definitions consequently refer to employed persons in the U.S. private domestic economy aged 16 and over, corresponding to the labor force definition subsequent to 1966. Prior to 1966, officers of proprietary corporations were classified as self-employed in the household survey. In the revision, commencing with the 1967 survey for 1966 data, all persons who classified themselves as self-employed in the class of worker question were reclassified as employees if their business was incorporated. Subsequent to 1966, entrepreneurial status is accorded only to workers in the noncorporate sector.[15] Two control totals are constructed for 1966 to chain-link the effects of the survey redefinitions of employment.

The employment totals provide the series for the construction of the index (2.8). The labor input index per employed person is derived from the construction of a cross-classification and through determination of shifts in the composition of employment over time. By weighting with relative shares, an index of the form (2.4) is derived, from which the quality index (2.6) can be constructed. The same cross-classification used for employment is applied to annual hours and total compensation. The employment cross-classification on which the labor input measure is based contains the factors age, class of worker, educational attainment, occupation, sex, and industry of employment. Relative shifts of employment toward high-wage categories increase labor input per person. The classification within the levels of these factors is complete and crossed. The within-industry factor levels and the industrial classification, summarized in Tables A-1 and A-2 of Appendix A, yield a total of 1400 categories within each of fifty-seven industries. Data on household classifications involving any combination of the six factors, including those with incomplete levels, are obtained from published frequency distributions. The sources for the 1947–1972 period are the censuses of 1950, 1960, and 1970 and the *CPS*. Given that the complete crossed six-way classification is not available in published form, a statistical match of data is performed from the marginal classifications.[16]

The algorithm used is a modified version of the biproportional procedure for estimating the array of elements required to construct the $N_{i,s}$ elements of (2.4). The objective is to seek a transformation of a given array satisfying various nonnegativity constraints.[17] The algorithm as used in the creation of data sets is illustrated in Figure 2.2. An initial value is selected for all cells in the six-way classification. The published control totals by level from marginal classifications involving at least one of the six given factors are the constraints to be satisfied by the final array of persons engaged. These marginal totals and the control total of persons engaged are inputs. The algorithm selects a series of premultiplier arrays satisfying the marginal constraints and nonnegativity of all elements, given a set of convergence criteria.

There are two modifications of the basic RAS procedure. First, any number of marginal classifications can be used as input, as opposed to the two classifications of the commonly used transactions RAS. The

**Figure 2.2.**  Modified Biproportional Employment Algorithm

| *Notation* | *Definition* |
| --- | --- |
| $E_i^{mn}$ | persons engaged array $(M \times 1)$ |
| $m$ | iteration superscript |
| $n$ | subscript for marginal array of constraints, $n = 1 \ldots N$ |
| $i$ | index set (six characteristics) |
| $F_j^n$ | marginal or constraint array, with index set, $J$, $J$ member of $M$ |
| $K_L, K_U$ | prespecified upper and lower bounds |

**Figure 2.2.**    (Continued)

| *Procedure* | *Comment* |
|---|---|
| 1.   Initialize $E_i^{00} = \overline{E}_i^{00}$ | If census year, initialize with unit elements. If intercensal year, initialize with interpolated final census values. |
| 2.   Read first marginal (constraint) array $F_j^1$ | Includes aggregate employment control total. Arrays in relative or absolute frequency form. |
| 3.   Construct premultiplier $$P_j^1 = \frac{M_j^1}{\sum_{i \neq j} E_i^{00}}$$ | For proportion distribution, $$\sum_{j \in 0} p_j^1 = 1$$ |
| 4.   Calculate updated array $$E_i^1 = p^1 E_i^0$$ | Premultiplier matrix diagonal of form $$p^1 = \begin{matrix} p_j & 0 \\ 0 & I \end{matrix}$$ where dimension of $I$ is $(M - J)$ set difference |
| 5.   Go to 2. Read second array and repeat through 4. Perform for all $N$ sets of constraints. One iteration. | |
| 6.   Repeat 2–5 until convergence achieved | |

*Convergence Criteria*

(a)  $\min\limits_{i} \dfrac{E_i^{m,N}}{E_i^{(m-1)N}} \leq \epsilon$       $\epsilon$ arbitrarily small

(b)  $\max\limits_{i} \dfrac{E_i^{mN} - E_i^{(m-1)N}}{E_i^{(m-1)N}}$       Stratification of all cells by size and test percentage change.

  where $i\epsilon[K_L, K_U] \leq \delta$       $\delta$ arbitrarily small

*General Form*

$$E_i^{mN} = p^{mN} E_i^{m(N-1)} = \prod_{n=1}^{m(N-1)} p^n E_i^{00}.$$

modified procedure considers the marginal arrays pairwise sequentially. Second, the equiproportional assumption, for a given pair of arrays, obtains within factor levels common to both arrays. A search is performed on the factor level inputs and RAS applied only on factors not held in common. There are two criteria used for convergence. First, the minimal ratio of the value of a given cell at two successive iterations must be less than or equal to a given constant.[18] Second, all cells are classified by size, and the largest percentage change within each class is tested.

Given that the three census years in the sample possess the most marginal information on factor classifications, these years are processed first. Between census years are initialized with interpolated values from the converged census results, and the marginal totals are incorporated for each year. This provides a trend where no factor information is available for a given year. The procedure is repeated for each year in the sample.[19] The computation is performed separately and annually for both household and establishment counts. The total of full-time and part-time persons engaged in each industry from the *NIPA* provides the employee establishment control total. For the household base, the *CPS* count of persons engaged in the labor force by sex is used as the control, accounting for the 1966 redefinition in coverage from persons 14 and over to persons 16 and over.

The reconciliation is performed by subtracting secondary jobs held in the private sector by multiple job holders, with processing of household classifications the method used to allocate jobs in the six-way classification.[20] As a consequence of the small number of unpaid absentees, no specific adjustment is made for this category (Denison 1974). Two separate arrays are constructed for 1960 and 1966 to chain-link the effects of Alaska and Hawaii statehood and the survey redefinitions.

## Annual Hours Worked

The existence of establishment and household surveys of employment leads also to differences in measurement of annual hours worked. The first consideration in the construction of annual hours series is consequently the reconciliation of these alternative survey data.

Household data on annual hours are derived from the *CPS* and census questionnaires. For a given survey week, employed persons report the number of hours actually worked, as opposed to hours usually worked or scheduled.[21] In the published frequency distributions, some individuals are reported as working zero hours. This is because the household definition for weeks includes all those in which a person did any work for pay or profit, including sick leave or paid vacations, or worked as an unpaid family worker.[22] This measure is termed weeks paid, as opposed to the weeks worked nomenclature of the household survey. The data on weeks paid per year refer to the year previous to that of the survey. As a consequence, total hours worked in a given year represent the product of hours worked per week paid in the current year and weeks paid in the previous year.

There are several advantages to such a definition of hours worked. First, hours paid but not worked, which are not associated with the production of goods and services, are excluded. In addition, lost hours that reflect unpaid absenteeism, industrial disputes, or bad weather are excluded for similar reasons. The lagging procedure assigns appropriate hours and weeks to the same year.

For the establishment series, the *BLS* publishes paid total hours for an industrial classification[23] within each industry. The difference between the establishment and household totals represents hours paid but not worked. Consequently, the establishment data represent jobs filled and hours paid per job filled, while the household data measure employment and hours worked per person.

A second consideration, related to the reconciliation of establishment and household series, is the allocation of hours worked by multiple job holders. In the household survey, all hours worked by multiple job holders are assigned to the industry or occupation of primary employment.[24] Consequently, a reallocation procedure is required to collect all secondary hours worked by individuals in primary employment in a given industry or occupation and to reassign these hours to the activities to which they correspond. For the establishment survey, no reallocation of this form is required, since these hours are assigned to the industry in which they are worked.

Annual hours represent the product of weekly hours and annual weeks. Data from the household survey on hours worked per week paid, in frequency form, involving any of the six characteristics, are used as input. Mean hours worked per week estimates are derived by fitting distributions to the published frequencies, using a multinomial maximum likelihood (MML) estimating procedure.[25] The algorithm for constructing hours worked per week is indicated in Figure 2.3. The first stage is the estimation of means for the observed frequency distributions, involving a subset of the included characteristics. The resulting means are multiplied by the converged employment estimate for similar characteristics, yielding initial input on total hours. In addition, BLS data on industry total hours are used as establish-

**Figure 2.3.**    Multinomial Algorithm and Hours Data Construction

| *Notation* | *Definition* |
| --- | --- |
| $n_j$ | number of observations in cell $j$ |
| $\mu_j$ | probability of an observation occurring in cell $j$ |
| $u_j$ | upper bound for the class interval of cell $j$ |
| $d_j$ | lower bound for the class interval of cell $j$ |
| $f(x)$ | density function fitted over entire distribution |

*Procedure*

1.  Fit multinomial distributions to estimate $\alpha$, mean hours worked from hours frequencies, by maximum likelihood (MML)

$$P = \frac{n!}{\prod\limits_{j=1}^{J} n_j!} \prod_{j=1}^{J} \mu_j^{n_j} = \frac{n!}{\prod\limits_{j=1}^{J} n_j!} \prod_{j=1}^{J} \left[ \int_{d_j}^{u_j} f(s; \alpha)\, dx \right] n_j$$

2.  Multiply $\alpha_i$, obtained for characteristics $i$, by converged employment value. Yields total hours.

3.  Use RAS procedure, with constraints from BLS controls for total hours. Initialize all cells with 40 hours times persons engaged total.

4.  Upon convergence, divide by persons engaged.

*Comment*

The distributional form of $f(\cdot)$ can be varied to suit data. Examples are the lognormal and normal distributions.

ment control totals. The biproportional procedure on hours is performed and, upon convergence, divided by the converged employment estimates cellwise. For weeks paid per year an analogous procedure is used, to construct mean weeks paid in each cell.

The reassignment of hours worked by multiple job holders, given the final hours results of Figure 2.3, is described in Figure 2.4. Conditional distributions of hours worked in secondary activity, given

**Figure 2.4.**   Multiple Job Holding Hours Adjustments

| *Procedure* | *Notation* |
|---|---|
| 1.  Fit conditional distributions of secondary hours, given industry, from multinomial algorithm MML. | $H^{km}$, $km = p$ (primary)<br>$s$ (secondary) |
| 2.  Obtain conditional distributions of employment in multiple job holding | $N^{km}$ |
| 3.  Total hours adjustment, industry $j$ | |
| *Total hours allocated, industry j* | $T_j$ |
| LESS:<br>Total secondary hours worked, given primary employment in industry $j$ | $-\sum_{j=1}^{n} H_j^{sp} N_j^{sp}$ |
| ADD:<br>Secondary hours worked in industry $j$, given primary employment in industry $j$ | $+ H_j^{sp} N_j^{sp}$ |
| ADD:<br>Secondary hours worked in industry $j$, given secondary employment in industry $j$ | $+ H_j^{ss} N_j^{ss}$ |
| *= Total hours worked, industry j* | $= \overline{T}_j$ |

industry or occupation of primary activity, are used in the reallocation. The procedure is described for industrial adjustments with the occupational adjustment being identical. The figure for total hours allocated is the industry-specific average hours estimate obtained from the procedure described in Figure 2.3. Total secondary hours worked by persons primarily engaged in each industry are subtracted, and all secondary hours worked within the industry are added. This corrects for the allocation of secondary hours of multiple job holders to the industry of primary employment. Finally, annual hours worked per person in each cell is the cellwise product of hours worked per week paid and weeks paid per year in the cell.

### Shares in Labor Compensation

The final stage in the measurement of labor input is the computation of total labor compensation for each cell in the classification, from which the shares used to aggregate the quantity growth rates are derived. This procedure is described in Figure 2.5, given the construction of the employment and annual hours series. Published frequency distributions of wages and salaries for wage and salary workers represent the primary data. Means are fitted to these distributions for various subsets of characteristics.[26]

The appropriate control totals are establishment total employee

**Figure 2.5.**    Computation of Shares in Labor Compensation

*Procedure*
1.  Run MML on frequency distributions of wages and salaries by characteristics. Compute statutory contributions by employers for
    a.  social security
    b.  unemployment insurance
    for each distribution.
2.  Multiply by converged employment with same characteristics.
3.  Run RAS, controlling to establishment (*NIPA*) total of employee compensation by industry. For employees only.
4.  Upon convergence, divide compensation of employees cellwise by total cell hours, yielding mean hourly wage.
5.  Construct shares, imputing self-employed wage as that of equivalent employee.

compensation series by industry from the *NIPA*. These series represent employer payroll costs, including wage and salary payments and employer contributions to statutory and nonstatutory benefit programs.[27] These supplementary benefits are not reported received by employees in the household survey. An allocation is made, using a rate calculator, for two statutory programs where annual rates are available, social security and unemployment compensation. These adjustments are added to the wages per annum, providing the basic input for the compensation computation.

The converged employment level is multiplied by wages by characteristic, and the biproportional procedure is used to adjust the total to the *NIPA* industry figure, thereby allocating the remaining employer supplements. The converged values of this procedure, when divided cellwise by the product of employment and hours worked, represent hourly user costs of labor. From the compensation series, the arithmetic shares required for the Törnqvist index can be performed.

This method yields cell-specific wages for employees. For self-employed workers, the wage of a corresponding worker, given sex, age, education, occupation, and industry of employment, is imputed as the wage per hour of labor services provided in unincorporated activity.[28] Thus, the calculation of entrepreneurial labor services can be performed.

### Empirical Results

The computed data are applied to the construction of Törnqvist indices of labor input, employment and mean annual hours, unweighted indices of these components, and labor input per person and per hour. The complete results are reported in Tables 2.1 through 2.3.

All results are based on a value of unity in 1958. Two separate arrays are constructed for 1960 and 1966. The first value for 1960 represents inclusion of Alaska and Hawaii, and the second excludes these states. Consequently, the second value is consistent with the previous series, pertaining only to the coterminous United States. The first value for 1966 excludes the adjustments in the household survey, while the second adjusts for these redefinitions. The second value is consequently consistent with the previous series.

**Table 2.1**    Employment Indices, U.S. Private Domestic Economy, 1947–1972

| Year | (1) Weighted | (2) Unweighted | (3) Quality [(1) ÷ (2)] |
|------|------|------|------|
| 1947 | .886851 | .960111 | .923697 |
| 1948 | .904129 | .970897 | .931231 |
| 1949 | .876815 | .941815 | .930984 |
| 1950 | .883544 | .952277 | .927823 |
| 1951 | .926082 | .988996 | .936385 |
| 1952 | .947050 | .990839 | .955806 |
| 1953 | .980155 | 1.015022 | .965649 |
| 1954 | .964640 | .986240 | .978098 |
| 1955 | .983374 | 1.004329 | .979135 |
| 1956 | 1.004929 | 1.022906 | .982426 |
| 1957 | 1.012441 | 1.023258 | .989429 |
| 1958 | 1.000000 | 1.000000 | 1.000000 |
| 1959 | 1.024235 | 1.028157 | .996185 |
| 1960 | 1.019064 | 1.039179 | .980643 |
| 1960[a] | 1.014805 | 1.034636 | .980643 |
| 1961 | 1.044953 | 1.033659 | 1.010926 |
| 1962 | 1.073998 | 1.051414 | 1.021480 |
| 1963 | 1.084844 | 1.062509 | 1.021021 |
| 1964 | 1.106379 | 1.085025 | 1.019681 |
| 1965 | 1.136338 | 1.119735 | 1.041828 |
| 1966 | 1.172476 | 1.161584 | 1.009377 |
| 1966[b] | 1.172489 | 1.161974 | 1.009377 |
| 1967 | 1.175357 | 1.162297 | 1.011237 |
| 1968 | 1.207049 | 1.189201 | 1.015008 |
| 1969 | 1.238646 | 1.225768 | 1.010506 |
| 1970 | 1.236697 | 1.231354 | 1.004339 |
| 1971 | 1.247529 | 1.227606 | 1.016229 |
| 1972 | 1.285643 | 1.263591 | 1.017452 |

[a]Excluding Alaska and Hawaii.
[b]Adjusted for survey redefinitions.

**Table 2.2**   Hours Worked per Person Indices, U.S. Private Domestic Economy, 1947–1972

| Year | (1) Weighted | (2) Unweighted | (3) Quality [(1) ÷ (2)] |
|------|--------------|----------------|--------------------------|
| 1947 | 1.025793 | 1.074625 | .954559 |
| 1948 | 1.011996 | 1.056265 | .058089 |
| 1949 | 1.002638 | 1.051104 | .953890 |
| 1950 | 1.021809 | 1.070123 | .954852 |
| 1951 | 1.050061 | 1.069405 | .981911 |
| 1952 | 1.040339 | 1.055701 | .985449 |
| 1953 | 1.012192 | 1.033778 | .979119 |
| 1954 | 1.007573 | 1.029895 | .978326 |
| 1955 | 1.031299 | 1.040863 | .989861 |
| 1956 | 1.037373 | 1.040596 | .996903 |
| 1957 | 1.019868 | 1.019613 | 1.000251 |
| 1958 | 1.000000 | 1.000000 | 1.000000 |
| 1959 | 1.011399 | 1.01537 | .996102 |
| 1960 | 1.044765 | 1.025361 | 1.018924 |
| 1960[a] | 1.044761 | 1.025400 | 1.018924 |
| 1961 | 1.005125 | 1.000928 | 1.004193 |
| 1962 | 1.010858 | 1.001816 | 1.009026 |
| 1963 | 1.012223 | 1.998538 | 1.013705 |
| 1964 | 1.010226 | .989070 | 1.021390 |
| 1965 | 1.022170 | 1.001200 | 1.020945 |
| 1966 | 1.019573 | .992559 | 1.027217 |
| 1966[b] | 1.019487 | .990727 | 1.027217 |
| 1967 | 1.025442 | 1.005381 | 1.019953 |
| 1968 | 1.024279 | 1.000904 | 1.023354 |
| 1969 | 1.023734 | .995607 | 1.028251 |
| 1970 | 1.007422 | .979126 | 1.028900 |
| 1971 | 1.007784 | .976906 | 1.031608 |
| 1972 | 1.007847 | .976809 | 1.031776 |

[a] Excluding Alaska and Hawaii.
[b] Adjusted for survey redefinitions.

**Table 2.3**   Total Hours Indices, U.S. Private Domestic Economy, 1947–1972

| Year | (1)<br>Weighted | (2)<br>Unweighted | (3)<br>Quality [(1) ÷ (2)] |
|------|------|------|------|
| 1947 | .909726 | 1.031759 | .881723 |
| 1948 | .914975 | 1.025524 | .892202 |
| 1949 | .879127 | .989946 | .888056 |
| 1950 | .902813 | 1.019053 | .885934 |
| 1951 | .972442 | 1.057638 | .919447 |
| 1952 | .985253 | 1.046030 | .941898 |
| 1953 | .992105 | 1.049308 | .935485 |
| 1954 | .971945 | 1.015724 | .956899 |
| 1955 | 1.014153 | 1.046373 | .969208 |
| 1956 | 1.042486 | 1.064431 | .979383 |
| 1957 | 1.032556 | 1.043327 | .989677 |
| 1958 | 1.000000 | 1.000000 | 1.000000 |
| 1959 | 1.035910 | 1.043947 | .992302 |
| 1960 | 1.064682 | 1.065534 | .999201 |
| 1960[a] | 1.060228 | 1.060916 | .999201 |
| 1961 | 1.050309 | 1.034618 | 1.015165 |
| 1962 | 1.085660 | 1.053323 | 1.030700 |
| 1963 | 1.098104 | 1.060956 | 1.034014 |
| 1964 | 1.117693 | 1.073166 | 1.041492 |
| 1965 | 1.161531 | 1.121078 | 1.036083 |
| 1966 | 1.195425 | 1.152940 | 1.036849 |
| 1966[b] | 1.195338 | 1.151199 | 1.036849 |
| 1967 | 1.205260 | 1.168552 | 1.031414 |
| 1968 | 1.236355 | 1.190275 | 1.038713 |
| 1969 | 1.268044 | 1.220384 | 1.039054 |
| 1970 | 1.245876 | 1.205650 | 1.033365 |
| 1971 | 1.257240 | 1.199257 | 1.048349 |
| 1972 | 1.295732 | 1.234286 | 1.049783 |

[a]Excluding Alaska and Hawaii.
[b]Adjusted for survey redefinitions.

Table 2.1 indicates the indices for share-weighted employment, unweighted employment, and labor input per employed person, or labor quality. The employment definition reported is for a reconciliation to the establishment-based data series. The Törnqvist index increases from .887 to 1.286 over the period, with the greater portion of the increase occurring after 1958. The sources of growth in each index are the growth rates of employment and quality per person. From columns (2) and (3), the dominant source of growth in labor input in the 1947–1958 period is quality per person, or the efficiency shift, while in the 1958–1972 period unweighted employment is dominant.

Annual hours data are represented in Table 2.2. The weighted hours index declines less than a corresponding unweighted index, as a consequence of an increase in efficiency per hour. The total hours indices are represented in the columns in Table 2.3, with the growth in labor input represented as the sum of the growth of employment, labor input per person, annual hours and labor input per hour. The growth sources breakdown is summarized in Table 2.4.

In the first period of the sample, 1947–1958, quality per person per hour is the dominant cause of the increase in labor input. The contribution of total hours is negative, given that the decrease in mean hours exceeds the increase in employment. Employment, as opposed to mean hours, is the greater contribution to labor input

**Table 2.4.**  Sources of Growth in Labor Input, 1947–1972

| Labor Input Component | 1947–1958 | 1958–1972 | 1947–1972 |
|---|---|---|---|
| Employment | 0.37 | 1.87 | 1.27 |
| Annual Hours per person | −0.68 | −0.19 | −0.39 |
| *Total Hours* | *−0.31* | *1.70* | *0.88* |
| Quality per person | 0.75 | 0.12 | 0.38 |
| Quality per hour | 0.44 | 0.23 | 0.30 |
| *Total Quality* | *1.19* | *0.35* | *0.68* |
| Labor input | 0.8 | 2.05 | 1.56 |

**Table 2.5.** Comparative Measures of Labor Input

| | Christensen-Jorgenson | Denison | Kendrick |
|---|---|---|---|
| 1. Employment Definition | BEA full-time equivalent employees and proprietors for nonfarm sector. Kendrick agricultural series. Private domestic economy, establishment-adjusted, 1947–1969. | Household-based business sector, U.S. Excludes households, governments, and institutions 1947–1969. | BEA full-time equivalent employees and nonfarm proprietors. USDA series on farm employment and household series on unpaid family workers, 1948–1969. |
| Index (unweighted) | .929–1.221 | .961–1.211 | .947–1.207 |
| 2. Mean Hours Definition | Establishment-based hours worked per job filled. Weeks per year constant. | Household-based hours worked per person. Adjusted for multiple job holders. Weeks per year constant. | Total hours by industry (BLS) divided by persons engaged. Establishment based. Weeks per year constant. |
| Index (unweighted) | 1.076–.995 | 1.068–.962 | 1.075–.998 |
| 3. Quality/Person/ Hours Definition | Changing composition by educational attainment, using median schooling years index of Griliches (1970). | Four separate components: (a) interactive age-sex composition; (b) educational composition, including quality of education; (c) efficiency per hour by specified intragroup changes; (d) efficiency per hour by specified intergroup changes. | Changing composition of manhours by industry. |
| Index | .895–1.090 | .912–1.050 | .967–1.036 |

growth. In the 1958–1972 period employment dominates quality, reversing the situation of the first period.

Alternative definitions of labor input components and derived results are presented in Table 2.5. The results reported are for the initial and terminal index values, with 1958 scaled at unity. The unweighted persons engaged and mean hours results are similar to those found in Table 2.1. The quality indices are dissimilar due to differences in procedure and construction.

### Conclusion

The measurement of labor input in the U.S. private domestic economy has been considered, with appropriate consistency adjustments made. Such issues as household and establishment series reconciliation, incomplete classifications, treatment of multiple job holders, and computation of full-cost wages arise in any data base for aggregate labor. As a consequence, identical procedures can be applied to a longer historical period than the 1947–1972 period considered here, as well as to other economic subsectors. In addition, such procedures can be applied internationally, to obtain comparative measures of labor input between countries.

From the empirical results, the observed increase in labor input for 1947–1958 is principally accounted for by quality change, while for 1958–1972 total hours are the dominant source. In both periods, the contribution of direct and compositional changes in employment exceed analogous changes for mean hours worked per person.

# 3

# SOURCES OF
# QUALITY CHANGE

Labor input is the product of total hours worked and average labor quality per hour. Labor quality accounts for the level of skill provided per hour worked, taking into account educational and demographic factors. Change in labor quality can be expressed as the sum of main effects associated with these factors and interactive effects of various orders yielding a growth accounting equation for labor input. This is applied to a classification of total hours worked by sex, class of worker (employee or self-employed), age, education, and occupation for the U.S. private domestic economy for the 1947–1974 period. The main conclusions are:

1.   The contribution to labor input growth of education is 0.6 percent per annum. This effect is reduced by one-half if interactive effects are included, as the educated become younger and more female. The main effect for education declines by over one-fifth between 1959–1963 and 1971–1974, which may indicate a decline in the contribution of education to U.S. productivity growth.

2.   A linear logarithmic quality change estimate excluding interactions overstates the growth of labor quality by one-half (Nelson 1973). This suggests that the contribution of education and experience to economic growth, for example, may not be measured by multiplying together indices of each factor. The overstatement amounts to 0.3 percent per annum, which at a labor share of two-thirds overstates the contribution of labor input to output growth by 0.2 percent per annum.

3.  The main effect of the substantial increase in the relative share of women in total hours is negative. The inclusion of interactive effects reduces the magnitude of this effect from $-.15$ to $-.07$ percent per annum, accounting for the skill composition of women.

4.  The 1959–1963 period is a watershed in terms of the relative importance of total hours and labor quality as sources of labor input growth. From 1947 to 1959, labor quality is relatively dominant, accounting for over three-quarters of labor input growth of about 1.3 percent per annum. For 1963–1974, labor input increases in growth to 1.9 percent annually, but quality change accounts for only one-tenth. Quality change in the U.S. labor market almost disappears, declining from 1.12 percent for 1947–1952 to 0.12 percent over 1971–74.

### Labor Input Indexing

The indexing of labor input commences with a production function aggregating nonlabor services and the services provided by different types of labor. An aggregate of labor input exists if types of labor are weakly separable from nonlabor inputs. In this circumstance, the relative wages of types of labor are unaffected by the levels on nonlabor inputs. Assume that the labor market is efficient and that types of labor are paid marginal products. Labor input can increase even if total hours worked remains constant. Suppose there are two types of labor, skilled and unskilled. The former receives above-average wages, yet both work the same hours. If an unskilled worker becomes skilled, total hours remains unchanged, but labor input increases since the marginal product of this worker increases. The objective is to quantify these changes in labor input and associate them with characteristics of employment.

The production function, separable into labor and nonlabor inputs, is at time t:

$$y_t = g(z_t, x_{1t}, \ldots, x_{pt}, t) \qquad (3.1)$$

where $y_t$ represents output, $z_t$ labor input, and $x_{1t}, \ldots, x_{pt}$ the services of nonlabor inputs.[1] The labor aggregate is

$$z_t = f(h_{1t}, \ldots, h_{lt}) \qquad (3.2)$$

where $h_{it}$, $i = 1, \ldots, I$ represents hours worked by type $i$ labor. Under efficient labor markets and linear homogeneity of $f$,

$$\frac{\partial \ln z_t}{\partial t} = \sum_{i=1}^{I} s_{it} \frac{\partial \ln h_{it}}{\partial t} \tag{3.3}$$

where

$$s_{it} = \partial \ln f / \partial \ln h_{it} = w_{it} h_{it} / \sum_{i=1}^{I} w_{it} h_{it} \tag{3.4}$$

represents the share of the ith type in total labor compensation. The hourly wage of the $i$th type is $w_{it}$, and its compensation $w_{it} h_{it}$. The growth rate of labor input is a convex combination of growth rates of total hours for each type of labor, with compensation shares as weights.

Total hours worked for all types of labor are $m_t = \Sigma_{i=1}^{I} h_{it}$, and the growth rate of these is

$$\frac{\partial \ln m_t}{\partial t} = \sum_{i=1}^{I} b_{it} \frac{\partial \ln h_{it}}{\partial t} \tag{3.5}$$

with $b_{it} = h_{it}/m_t$ the share of total hours worked by the $i$th labor type. Average labor quality per hour is labor input divided by total hours worked:

$$a_t = z_t / m_t \tag{3.6}$$

and its growth rate is

$$\frac{\partial \ln a_t}{\partial t} = \sum_{i=1}^{I} (s_{it} - b_{it}) \frac{\partial \ln h_{it}}{\partial t} \tag{3.7}$$

at time $t$. This growth rate is termed "quality change" and is the sum of growth rates of hours worked by each type of labor, weighted by the difference between the shares in labor compensation and hours worked.

The labor aggregate is specified to have the translog form

$$\ln z_t = \alpha_0 + \sum_{i=1}^{I} \alpha_i \ln h_{it} + 1/2 \sum_{i=1}^{I} \sum_{j=1}^{I} \beta_{ij} \ln h_{it} \ln h_{jt} \tag{3.8}$$

where $\alpha_0$, $\alpha_i$, $i = 1, \ldots, I$ and $\beta_{ij}$, $i, j = 1, \ldots, I$ are parameters and where $\beta_{ij} = \beta_{jt}$.[2] Under linear homogeneity, $\Sigma_{i=1}^{I} \alpha_i = 1$ and $\Sigma_{j=1}^{I} \beta_{ij} =$

$0, i = 1, \ldots, I$. Efficiency requires the relative share of the $i$th type of labor to be equal to its logarithmic marginal product, or

$$s_{it} = \alpha_i + \sum_{j=1}^{I} \beta_{ij} \ln h_{jt} \qquad (3.9)$$

where the $s_{it}$ are as defined in (3.4). Equations (3.8) and (3.9) plus the symmetry conditions $\beta_{ij} = \beta_{ji}$ imply

$$d_t = \sum_{i=1}^{I} v_{it} \Delta \ln h_{it} \qquad (3.10)$$

for the logarithmic first difference $d_t \equiv \Delta \ln z_t$, where $\Delta$ denotes the first-difference operator and $v_{it} = 1/2(s_{it} + s_{i,t+1})$. This is the growth rate of the translog index of labor input.[3]

The growth of hours worked is defined in discrete time by

$$h_t \equiv \Delta \ln m_t \qquad (3.11)$$

and the growth rate for quality change in discrete time is

$$q_t \equiv d_t - h_t \qquad (3.12)$$

where $d_t$ is defined by (3.10) and $h_t$ by (3.11). If hours of relatively high wage labor increase more rapidly than total hours, $q_t$ is positive.

In the labor market, a series of employment characteristics is observable and determines the marginal product of each worker. Suppose there are n factors, and the inputs are classified mutually exclusively and exhaustively into the levels of these factors. The growth of labor input is, deleting the time subscript,

$$d = \sum_{i(1)=1}^{I(1)} \cdots \sum_{i(n)=1}^{I(n)} v_i(1), \ldots, i(n)\Delta \ln hi(1), \ldots, i(n) \qquad (3.13)$$

where the factors $j = 1, \ldots, n$ are classified into levels $I(1), \ldots, I(n)$. Labor input growth is the weighted sum over cell configurations $i(1)$, $\ldots, i(n)$. The aggregate quality change is decomposable into characteristic sources through the use of partial indices of labor input.[4]

A growth rate of a partial labor input index involves share weighting over a proper subset of the factors $j = 1, \ldots, n$. A partial translog growth rate uses the $v_i$ of the factors included in the subset, constructed by arithmetic mean share weighting. Labor is regarded as being homogeneous (i.e., wage rates are identical) over the factors that are not included in the subset. If the growth of total hours is subtracted, the contribution to quality change of the factor subset is obtained, assuming (possibly erroneously) that labor is homogeneous over the factors not included in the subset.

The growth rate of the partial index including a single factor is

$$d_1 = \sum_{i(1)=1}^{I(1)} v_i(1) \Delta \ln \left[ \sum_{i(2)=1}^{I(2)} \cdots \sum_{i(n)=1}^{I(n)} h_i(2), \ldots, i(n) \right] \quad (3.14)$$

where $d_1$ is the growth rate and the factors are renumbered such that the considered factor is the first. Unweighted summation of total hours occurs over the last $(n-1)$ factors, and the share weight $v_{i(1)}$ is constructed by summation within the level $i(1)$ over the levels of the remaining factors. The growth rate is of a partial information form in that share weighting occurs only over the levels of the first factor.

The growth rate of a partial index of the first $j$ factors is

$$d_{1,\ldots,j} = \sum_{i(1)=1}^{I(1)} \cdots \sum_{i(j)=1}^{I(j)} v_{i(1),\ldots,i(j)} \Delta \ln \left[ \sum_{i(j+1)=1}^{I(j+1)} \cdots \sum_{i(n)=1}^{I(n)} h_{i(j+1),\ldots,i(n)} \right] (3.15)$$

where the shares $v_{i(1),\ldots,i(j)}$ are constructed by summation over the remaining $(n-j)$ factors within the cell configuration $i(1), \ldots, i(j)$. Each of the partial index growth rates $d_{1,\ldots,j}$ can be justified in the context of the translog aggregation exactly as in (3.8) through (3.10), except for the assumption that the wage restriction

$$w_{i(1),\ldots,i(j),i(j+1),\ldots,i(n)} = w_{i(1),\ldots,i(j),k(j+1),\ldots,k(n)}$$

for any $i(j+1), \ldots, i(n)$ and $k(j+1), \ldots, k(n)$ is required.

By this procedure growth rates and partial indices of quality change for all proper subsets of the labor characteristics are derived. The partial indices provide a structure for the source decomposition of quality change. The main effect of factor $i$, or efficiency adjustment to total hours, is the difference between the growth of its single factor index $d_i$ and total hours. This yields

$$q_i = d_i - h \quad (3.16)$$

where $q_i$ is the main effect of factor $i$. If $q_i$ is positive, then this main effect augments total hours. Labor input constructed as the sum of hours worked is biased downward.[5]

If there are two factors, $i$ and $k$, that form a proper subset from $n$ factors, a first-order interactive effect is derived from the partial index growth rate $d_{ik}$ for the two factors and the single factor indices $d_i$ and $d_k$. The first-order interactive effect between $i$ and $k$ is

$$q_{ik} = (d_{ik} - h) - (d_i - h) - (d_k - h)$$
$$= d_{ik} - h - q_i - q_k \tag{3.17}$$

as the total joint effect of $i$ and $k$ or $(d_{ik} - h)$ less the main effect of each. If there are only two factors, quality change is

$$q = d_{ik} - h$$
$$= q_i + q_k + q_{ik} \tag{3.18}$$

the sum of the main effects and the interaction. From the $d_{1,\ldots,j}$, interactive effects up to $(j-1)$th order are obtainable. In a four-factor classification, effects up to third order are derived, and quality change is

$$q = d_{1,\ldots,4} - h$$
$$= \sum_{i=1}^{4} q_i + \sum_{i=1}^{4} \sum_{j=i+1}^{4} q_{ij} \tag{3.19}$$
$$+ \sum_{i=1}^{4} \sum_{j=i+1}^{4} \sum_{k=j+1}^{4} q_{ijk} + q_{1234}$$

where $q_{1234}$ is the third-order interaction.

A numerical example detailing the procedure and the errors resulting from incorrect specification is given in Table 3.1. Panel A presents a classification by education when age, another determinant of labor input, is omitted. Labor input grows at 9.39 percent over the period, and $q_1 = d_1 - h = .0294$ is the education effect. When the correct and complete data of panel B are used, labor input growth is $d_{12}$ or 10.67 percent, indicating that a downward bias of 13.6 percent arises from the incorrect exclusion of age.

The analogous age effect is $q_2 = d_2 - h = .0030$, so the shifting age composition increases labor input by 0.3 percent. The education-age interaction is $q_{12} = d_{12} - d_1 - d_2 - h = .0098$, indicating that this effect adds to labor input. The sources of growth in labor input are: total hours worked, 6.45 percent; changing educational composition, 2.94

**Table 3.1.**  Quality Change Data, One- and Two-Factor Examples

### A. One Factor, Education

| Time (t) | College (C) | | High School (H) | |
|---|---|---|---|---|
| | Total hours (billion) | Wage/hour ($) | Total hours (billion) | Wage/hour ($) |
| t | 10 | 5 | 20 | 3 |
| t + 1 | 12 | 7 | 20 | 3 |

$v_C = (.45 + .58)/2 = .515$

$v_H = (.55 + .42)/2 = .485$

$d_1 = .515 \times .1823 = .0939$

$\Delta \ln h_C = \ln 12 - \ln 10 = .1823$

$\Delta \ln h_H = \ln 20 - \ln 20 = 0$

$h = \ln 32 - \ln 30 = .0645$

**Table 3.1.** (Continued)

### B. Two Factors, Education and Age

| | College, Under 30 (C,U) | | College, Over 30 (C,A) | |
|---|---|---|---|---|
| | Total hours (billion) | Wage/hour ($) | Total hours (billion) | Wage/hour ($) |
| $t$ | 2 | 5 | 8 | 5 |
| $t+1$ | 3 | 7 | 9 | 7 |
| | High School, Under 30 (H,U) | | High School, Over 30 (H,A) | |
| $t$ | 5 | 2 | 15 | 3.33 |
| $t+1$ | 4 | 2 | 16 | 3.25 |

$$v_{C,U} = .12$$
$$v_{C,A} = .40$$
$$v_{H,U} = .07$$
$$v_{H,A} = .41$$
$$v_U = .19$$
$$v_A = .81$$
$$d_2 = .81 \times .0834 = .0675$$
$$d_{12} = (.12 \times .4055) + (.40 \times .1178) + (.07 \times -.2231) + (.41 \times .0645) = .0675$$

$$\Delta \ln h_{C,U} = .4055$$
$$\Delta \ln h_{C,A} = .1178$$
$$\Delta \ln h_{H,U} = -.2231$$
$$\Delta \ln h_{H,A} = .0645$$
$$\Delta \ln h_U = 0$$
$$\Delta \ln h_H = \ln 25 - \ln 23 = .0834$$

percent; age composition, 0.03 percent; and education-age interaction, 0.98 percent. With a linear logarithmic aggregate, the interaction would be restricted to zero and labor input growth would be biased downward, relative to $d_{12}$, by 9 percent.[6]

More generally, interactions in an $n$ factor classification are constructed analogously as marginal contributions given total hours, all main effects, and all interactions up to order $n - 1$. Quality change is a growth accounting identity, being the sum of main effects for each factor and interactive effects involving subsets of factors.

### Data Construction

The structure is applied to a complete crossed classification of total hours worked and average wages per hour in the U.S. private domestic economy for the 1947–1974 period. There are 1,600 types of labor, classified by factor and level in Table 3.2. (This classification differs slightly from that in Table A.1, Appendix A.) There are five educational groups, eight age groups, ten occupations (one digit), and two classes of worker for each sex. The data are described briefly here; more detail is provided in Gollop and Jorgenson (1980).

The data are controlled to match series on total jobs filled and hours worked published by the Bureau of Economic Analysis (BEA) of the U.S. Department of Commerce in its *Survey of Current Business*. These data are based on payroll records reported to state unemployment insurance bureaus and do not include information on the relevant employment characteristics.

These characteristics of class, sex, age, education, and occupation, together with industry information, are obtained from household surveys of the labor force, published in the decennial census and the *Current Population Survey* (*CPS*). The industry classification is almost identical to that for the BEA; it contains fifty-one sectors with 1,600 types of labor in each, or a total of 81,600 groups. Published cross-tabulations are available for subsets of the factors but not for the entire classification. The objective is to combine the available partial classifications to construct the 1,600 types of labor for each industry and year.

The procedure is summarized in Table 3.3. All partial classifications on persons employed for each year are obtained; for example,

**Table 3.2.**    Classification of Labor Input

*Education*

    Elementary (0–8 years of elementary school)
    Some high school (1–3 years of high school)
    High school graduate
    Some college (1–3 years of college)
    College graduate (4 years or more of college)

*Sex*

    Male
    Female

*Age*

    14–15, 16–17, 18–24, 25–34, 35–44, 45–54, 55–64, 65 and above

*Class of Worker*

    Private wage and salary employee
    Self-employed or unpaid family worker

*Occupation*

    Professional, technical, and kindred
    Managerial
    Farm and farm managerial
    Clerical
    Sales
    Service (including private household workers)
    Operative
    Crafts
    Farm laborer
    Laborer

two-way sex-age or sex-occupation tables. These are multiplied together using a multivariate version of the biproportional algorithm of Bacharach (1965) and controlled to BEA jobs filled. This yields series on jobs filled for all 1,600 labor groups.

Hours worked per job are published as frequency distributions in the census and *CPS*. Mean hours worked per job are estimated for all available partial classifications. The jobs filled series is summed to be consistent with these mean hours. If mean hours worked by sex and occupation are available, total hours worked are obtained by multiplying jobs filled summed over class, education and age, and

**Table 3.3.**  Labor Input Data Construction by Industry

|  |  | Source |
| --- | --- | --- |
| Operation (on opposite item) | (1)  Employment | |
| Control to | Persons employed (partial) Jobs filled | Census, *CPS* BEA |
| = | Jobs filled (1,600 types) (1) | |
| | (2)  Hours worked | |
| | Mean hours worked/job (partial) | Census, *CPS* |
| × | Jobs filled (see (1)) | |
| = | Total hours worked (partial) | |
| Control to | Total hours worked | BEA |
| = | Total hours worked (1,600 types) | |
| Divide by | Jobs filled (1,600 types) (1) | |
| = | Mean jobs/worked/job (1,600 types) | |
| | (3)  Weeks paid: Jobs per person | |
| | Mean weeks paid/worker (partial) | Census, *CPS* |
| Divide by | Fifty-two weeks | |
| = | Mean jobs/worker (partial) | |
| × | Jobs filled (see (1)) | |
| Multiply Together | | |
| = | Total jobs/worker (1,600 cells) (3) | |
| Multiply by | Fifty-two weeks | |
| = | Mean weeks paid/worker (1,600 cells) (3) | |
| | (4)  Hourly user cost of labor (employees) | |
| | Mean earnings/worker-year (partial) | Census, *CPS* |
| Add | Social Security and unemployment insurance | |
| = | Mean adjusted earnings/ worker-year (partial) | |

Table 3.3.    Continued

| | | Source |
|---|---|---|
| Divide by | Total jobs/worker (1,600 cells) (3) | |
| = | Mean adjusted earnings/job (partial) | |
| × | Jobs filled (see (1)) | |
| = | Total adjusted earnings (partial) | |
| Control to | Wages plus supplements | BEA |
| = | Total earnings (1,600 cells) | |
| Divide by | Hours worked/job (see (2)) | |
| × | Jobs filled (see (1)) | |
| Multiply by | Fifty-two weeks | |
| = | Mean user cost per hour | |

mean hours. These are controlled to BEA series on total hours worked.

A job is any activity providing fifty-two weeks of paid employment during a year. What are reported in household surveys as weeks worked include sick leave and vacation, so the actual series is weeks paid. The procedures for constructing series on weeks paid are analogous to those for hours worked per job, except that there is no BEA control total on weeks paid by industry. Given the definition of a job, jobs per worker are weeks paid divided by fifty-two.

It is assumed that marginal products of employees are equated with the user cost of labor. The user cost is the wage rate plus any hourly related wage supplements. Means are estimated for earnings frequency distributions for employees, with the algorithm containing a tax calculator to add employer contributions to Social Security and payroll unemployment insurance. The biproportional procedure is used to construct total earnings, inclusive of employer supplements, for all 800 types of employees. This total is divided by the product of hours worked per job, jobs filled, and fifty-two to yield the mean user cost of labor.

For the 800 self-employed cells, total labor compensation must be imputed. The after-tax rate of return on capital is assumed equal in the corporate and noncorporate sectors. This return is multiplied by noncorporate capital stock to yield an estimate of noncorporate capital income. This is subtracted, by industry, from noncorporate income to yield noncorporate labor income. Since hours worked per job and jobs filled can be estimated as explained in Table 3.3, imputed hourly wage rates for all 800 cells can be constructed.

The relevant wages $w_i, i = 1, \ldots, 1,600$ are the user costs of labor for employees and the self-employed, with compensation, hours, and employment summed over industry. Total hours $h_i$ are the product of jobs filled, mean hours worked per job, and fifty-two. Labor compensation shares are

$$s_i = w_i h_i / \sum_{i-1}^{1600} w_i h_i$$

calculated annually for 1947–1974. The $v_i$ are constructed as two-year moving averages of the $s_i$.


### Empirical Results

The results of the quality change decomposition are presented, and the magnitudes of factor effects discussed and compared with alternative estimates. The sum of the interactions is examined to determine whether labor quality can be represented by a main effects or linear logarithmic index. Marginal quality contributions are computed for specific factors, given the four remaining factors, and these are compared with the main effects.

The quality change decomposition for all effects and interactions is presented in Table 3.4. Quality change is the sum of five main effects and twenty-six interactions (ten of first order, ten of second order, five of third order, and one of fourth order). For the 1947–1951 period quality change or growth in labor input per hour worked averages 1.12 percent per annum. Quality change exhibits fluctuations over the period, declining to $-0.23$ percent during 1963–1967, largely because of substantial negative main effects attributable to age and sex. That is, since negative effects arise when low-wage employment increases more rapidly than high wage employment, the decline is attributable to increasing shares of total hours worked for young workers and women.

The linear logarithmic quality growth rate is the sum of main effects only and averages 0.90 percent over the 1947–1974 period, as opposed to 0.60 percent when interactions are taken into account. This creates an upward bias of 50 percent if the linear logarithmic specification is used, overstating the rate of growth of labor input. Comparing the main effects, the overall contribution of sex composition is to reduce growth in labor input per hour by 0.15 percent per annum. Star (1974) has obtained an estimate of −0.01 percent for an analogous main effect of sex for 1950–1960.[7] In the 1951–1959 period, the quality change sex effect is −.026 percent. Barger (1971) obtains a main effect for sex for U.S. manufacturing, 1948–1966, of −0.24 percent, similar to the derived result. Both measures are based on similar arithmetic share weighting.

A watershed develops in the main effect of age within the period as age becomes a retarding factor after 1955–1959. The increase in the share of total hours worked by younger workers decreases the main effect, but for the period as a whole the effect of age is close to zero. The main effect of class is positive at 0.15 percent, accounting for the decline in the relative share of hours worked by the self-employed. Denison (1974) estimates that for the U.S. business sector, 1950–1962, the movement of all resources from noncorporate to corporate sectors increases output per capita by 0.29 percent, not inconsistent with the results obtained here.[8]

The education effect increases monotonically to 0.85 percent from 1963 to 1967, but with the decline in relative wages of the college educated outweighing their increasing share of total hours, the effect is 0.67 percent for 1971–1974. A single-factor education index in Christensen and Jorgenson (1973) yields 0.71 percent for the U.S. private domestic economy, 1947–1969. Denison derives an estimate of 0.65 percent for the U.S. business sector, 1947–1969.[9] These estimates are similar to the result obtained. The latter measure includes a correction for the quality of schooling through the use of length of school year as a classifying variable.

Waldorf (1973) obtains an estimate of 0.32 percent for labor quality change in U.S. manufacturing by occupation, 1952–1967, using arithmetic share weighting. The occupational effect becomes negative at −0.11 percent for 1971–1974, indicating that the growing job opportunities in this period occur among those with relatively low wages.

Among the first-order interactions, that for sex and age is negligible, indicating a proportionate increase in employment among

**Table 3.4.** Quality Change Decomposition, U.S. Private Domestic Economy, 1947–1974 (average percent per year)

| | 1947–74 | 1947–51 | 1951–55 | 1955–59 | 1959–63 | 1963–67 | 1967–71 | 1971–74 |
|---|---|---|---|---|---|---|---|---|
| *Main Effects* | | | | | | | | |
| Sex (S) | −.15 | .04 | −.19 | −.34 | −.05 | −.24 | −.22 | −.06 |
| Class (C) | .14 | .28 | .13 | .26 | .14 | .04 | .05 | .09 |
| Age (A) | −.01 | .34 | .27 | .03 | −.07 | −.22 | −.20 | −.29 |
| Education (E) | .61 | .27 | .50 | .58 | .72 | .85 | .81 | .67 |
| Occupation (J) | .31 | .63 | .32 | .42 | .37 | .14 | .40 | −.11 |
| | .90 | 1.56 | 1.03 | .95 | 1.11 | .57 | .84 | .30 |
| *Interactive Effects* | | | | | | | | |
| *First Order* | | | | | | | | |
| SC | .05 | .05 | .00 | .01 | .14 | .17 | .00 | .02 |
| SA | .02 | −.07 | −.02 | −.03 | .13 | .12 | .02 | −.01 |
| SE | .07 | .03 | .06 | .09 | .13 | .13 | .03 | .02 |
| SJ | .09 | −.01 | .12 | .17 | .17 | .15 | .07 | −.03 |
| CA | .04 | .07 | .06 | .02 | .12 | .04 | −.01 | −.03 |
| CE | −.05 | −.03 | −.04 | −.05 | .06 | −.20 | −.04 | −.02 |
| CJ | −.10 | −.10 | −.06 | −.12 | .07 | −.51 | .03 | −.05 |
| AE | .02 | .01 | .05 | .00 | .12 | .03 | −.01 | −.07 |
| AJ | .00 | −.10 | −.04 | −.04 | .09 | .00 | .04 | .06 |
| EJ | −.27 | −.22 | −.30 | −.41 | −.18 | −.36 | −.35 | −.05 |
| | −.13 | −.37 | −.17 | −.36 | .85 | −.43 | −.22 | −.16 |

**Table 3.4.**  (Continued)

| | 1947–74 | 1947–51 | 1951–55 | 1955–59 | 1959–63 | 1963–67 | 1967–71 | 1971–74 |
|---|---|---|---|---|---|---|---|---|
| *Second Order* | | | | | | | | |
| SCA | -.03 | -.01 | -.01 | -.01 | -.09 | -.07 | -.00 | -.01 |
| SCE | -.03 | .00 | .01 | .00 | -.10 | -.11 | -.00 | -.01 |
| SCJ | -.06 | -.06 | -.00 | -.01 | -.15 | -.20 | .01 | -.01 |
| SAE | -.02 | -.01 | -.02 | -.02 | -.09 | .00 | .02 | .01 |
| SAJ | -.02 | .02 | -.01 | -.01 | -.09 | -.07 | .00 | -.01 |
| SEJ | -.07 | -.03 | -.03 | -.06 | -.17 | -.12 | -.05 | -.04 |
| CAE | .00 | .01 | .03 | .03 | -.06 | -.02 | .02 | .02 |
| CAJ | -.03 | -.04 | -.03 | -.02 | -.11 | .00 | -.01 | .01 |
| CEJ | .01 | .02 | .04 | .05 | -.08 | .04 | -.01 | -.02 |
| AEJ | -.01 | .02 | .03 | .05 | -.12 | -.05 | -.01 | .02 |
| | -.27 | -.08 | -.01 | .00 | -1.06 | -.60 | -.03 | -.04 |
| *Third Order* | | | | | | | | |
| SCAE | .02 | .01 | .00 | .00 | .11 | .03 | .00 | .00 |
| SCAJ | .02 | .01 | .01 | .01 | .10 | .04 | .00 | .01 |
| SCEJ | .03 | .00 | -.01 | .00 | .10 | .13 | .00 | .00 |
| SAEJ | .03 | .01 | .02 | .02 | .10 | .03 | -.01 | .01 |
| CAEJ | .01 | -.01 | .00 | -.02 | -.02 | .07 | .03 | .00 |
| | .11 | .02 | .00 | .01 | .48 | .26 | -.01 | .02 |
| *Fourth Order* | | | | | | | | |
| SCAEJ | -.02 | -.01 | .00 | .00 | -.11 | -.03 | .00 | .00 |
| Quality Change | .60 | 1.12 | .85 | .60 | 1.27 | -.23 | .58 | .12 |
| Total Hours | .86 | .59 | .29 | .29 | -.03 | 2.54 | .26 | 2.55 |
| *Labor Input* | *1.46* | *1.71* | *1.14* | *.89* | *1.24* | *2.31* | *.84* | *2.67* |

women in all age groups. The remaining age interactions with class, education, and occupation are all close to zero. Consequently, the relative increase in the proportion of total hours worked by younger workers is not concentrated in any given skill class. In no case is any age interaction of substantial magnitude.

The interactions of sex with education and occupation are 0.07 and 0.09 percent, respectively, from 1947 to 1974, implying that the proportion of women has increased more rapidly in the skilled labor categories. These two first-order interactions alone eliminate the entire main effect of −0.15 percent per year and amount to over one-quarter of the 1947–1974 quality change. Moveover, the interaction with class is positive at 0.05 percent per year, implying that women have shifted more rapidly than men from self-employment, including unpaid family workers, to employees. Quality change constructed by main effects summation overstates the reduction in labor input through increases in female employment.

The class interactions with education and occupation are both negative, indicating that employees are concentrated in high-wage, higher education, and skilled occupation groups. The education and occupation interaction is negative, at −0.27 percent over the period. High-wage groups, one-to-three years of college, and college graduates in educational attainment, are also in skilled occupations. The interaction reduces the effect of education and occupation from 0.92 percent per annum to 0.65 percent.

The interactions of higher order are of small magnitude but their sum is consistently negative. The largest effect is the education-sex-occupation interaction, given that high-wage education-sex groups have high proportions of total hours worked by persons in relatively high-wage occupations.

The last three entries in the rows of Table 3.4 correspond to $q_t$, $h_t$, and $d_t$, the growth rates of labor input per hour worked, total hours worked, and labor input. There is a role reversal between quality change and total hours as sources of growth during the period. The average quality change in the period, 1947–1951, amounts to 1.12 percent with a positive sex effect associated with increasing male employment share. This rate of growth declined to 0.12 percent by 1971–1974, mainly attributable to rapid growth in low-wage occupations and shifts towards a younger work force.[10] The 1959–1963 period marks the turning point. During 1947–1963 the principal source of labor input growth is quality change, while for 1963–1974 total hours become dominant. Hours worked exhibit a relatively slow increase up to 1963 and a rapid increase thereafter. Whereas for 1947–1974 quality change accounts for 31 percent of the growth in labor input, the proportion is less than 4 percent after 1971.

The sum of the main effects elements yields the estimate of quality change consistent with linear logarithmic aggregation. The use of such a form overstates the quality measure, with the exception of the period 1963–1967. When quality change is positive, the main effects growth rate exceeds total quality change, implying that a linear logarithmic aggregation yields upward biases. The major interactive effects are those of second order, and the total of these has sign opposite to that of the main effects sum. This is a consequence of positive correlation between factor effects.

The marginal effect is the change in the labor input growth rate formed from $(n - 1)$ factors when the nth is added. The interactive effect is the sum of interactions of all orders containing this factor and is the difference between the marginal and main effects. The results of this procedure are presented in Table 3.5, where the marginal effect is the first entry, and the sum of the interactive effects the second entry. The main effect shown in Table 3.4 plus the interactive effect is the marginal effect. The marginal effect for sex exceeds the main effect, given the above-average increase in women in skilled labor types as indicated by the positive interaction effect. Main effects or linear logarithmic analysis of sex composition as a source of quality change overstates the decline in quality associated with the entry of women. The increase in the proportion of total hours worked by women increases the skill content of the average hour, given the positive sex interactions with education and occupation. The effect of the adjustment for interactive effects is to reduce the negative contribution of sex from $-0.15$ to $-0.07$ percent, or by about one-half, over the entire period.

The marginal effect of class for 1947–1974 is close to zero, implying that the relative decline of self-employment is captured by the levels of the remaining four characteristics. The age marginal effect is also close to zero for the entire period, although declining after the watershed period of 1959–1963. The interactive effect of

**Table 3.5.**  Factor Contributions to Quality Change, U.S. Private Domestic Economy, 1947–1974 (percent per year)

|  | 1947–51 | 1951–55 | 1955–59 | 1959–63 | 1963–67 | 1967–71 | 1971–74 | 1947–74 |
|---|---|---|---|---|---|---|---|---|
| *Sex* | | | | | | | | |
| Marginal | −.07 | −.09 | −.18 | .12 | −.05 | −.14 | −.08 | −.07 |
| Interactive | −.11 | .10 | .16 | .17 | .19 | .08 | −.02 | .08 |
| *Class* | | | | | | | | |
| Marginal | .17 | .09 | .13 | .19 | −.61 | .04 | .00 | .01 |
| Interactive | −.11 | −.04 | −.13 | .05 | −.65 | −.01 | −.09 | −.13 |
| *Age* | | | | | | | | |
| Marginal | .23 | .29 | .01 | .08 | −.15 | −.16 | −.21 | .02 |
| Interactive | −.11 | .02 | −.02 | .15 | .07 | .04 | .08 | .03 |
| *Education* | | | | | | | | |
| Marginal | .05 | .30 | .25 | .49 | .38 | .39 | .41 | .34 |
| Interactive | −.22 | −.20 | −.33 | −.23 | −.47 | −.42 | −.26 | −.27 |
| *Occupation* | | | | | | | | |
| Marginal | .20 | .28 | .08 | .05 | −.79 | .10 | −.15 | −.09 |
| Interactive | −.43 | −.04 | −.34 | −.32 | −.93 | −.30 | −.04 | −.41 |

age is negligible throughout, suggesting that linear logarithmic aggregation with a main effect only is appropriate for this factor.

The marginal effect of education is 0.34 percent, the additional contribution of this factor to an index already containing sex, class, age, and occupation. This is about one-half the main effect of education, implying that this portion is measurable by a linear combination of the remaining characteristics. The marginal effect of occupation is substantially less than the main effect. The inclusion of sex, class, education, and age interaction reduces the contribution of occupation from 0.32 to $-0.09$ percent over the period.

The measured effects of altering the sequence of entering factors differ considerably. This is because of the magnitude of the interaction terms. If education is added to the index after occupation, the negative effect of the first-order interaction reduces the contribution of education to labor input.

## Summary and Conclusions

Estimates of sources of quality change in labor input have been derived using the results of linkages among specification of the underlying functional form, index numbers corresponding to the form, and separability of labor from other factors of production. The separability assumption permits construction of measures of labor productivity without recourse to interaction between labor and nonlabor inputs. Such separability should be tested in expansion of consideration to nonlabor inputs. The functional form used, the translog, has the property of approximate consistency in aggregation. This implies that little error arises from a two-stage construction of value added through construction of subaggregates of labor and nonlabor inputs and subsequent aggregation of the two. This vitiates in large part any error from incorrect aggregation if separability does not obtain. Further work is required on the structure of the effects themselves. While no statistical testing is possible, the number of effects can be truncated at the first-order level if the aggregate of effects is translog. This yields a complete theory of labor productivity and hedonic labor indices connected with appropriate functional forms.

It has been demonstrated that the effect on reduced labor quality of increased female hours relative to male hours subsequent to World War II has been overstated. The results obtained indicate a negligible negative contribution before adjustments of relative wages by sex for discrimination or imperfect information.

The underlying contribution of education is reduced by one-half once adjustments are made for skill composition. Moreover, the main effect of education, although positive, declines by one-fifth from the early 1960s to the early 1970s. This reduction of 0.18 percent in the main effect of education would alone reduce output growth by 0.13 percent per year for a labor share of two-thirds. The evidence is that the large increases in employment shares of the relatively educated are failing to maintain the rise in productivity growth of the postwar era. Further examination of the return on investment in education is required.

Difficulties are posed in constructing labor input data consistent with the national accounts, and these problems are by no means resolved. The *CPS* survey week may be unrepresentative of the year. Wage data cannot accurately be attributed to each type of labor, and the biproportional procedure imparts an inflexibility in the allocation of labor that demands empirical testing.

The results depend on which classification is used, and the 1,600 types of labor are not exhaustive. Also, further work is required to determine whether user costs and marginal products are equated in the labor market, and whether observed wages include the effects of market distortions.

# 4

# LABOR SKILLS AND PRODUCTIVITY MEASUREMENT

Certain employment characteristics such as higher education or skilled occupation are associated with higher earnings. To determine appropriate investment levels in education or occupational training, a more relevant consideration is the contribution to output per hour worked, or labor productivity. This requires a general specification of technology to include contributions of various employment characteristics.

Productivity growth has been explained as attributable to various sources. Specifically, total factor productivity or output per unit of inputs has been decomposed into growth rates of aggregate inputs of capital and labor (Solow 1957; Jorgenson and Griliches 1967, 1972). The sources of growth methodology is extended here to focus on employment characteristics in order to explain labor input and labor productivity growth. Within this structure the effect of labor market policies on output per hour can be analyzed.

Labor productivity is decomposed into three sources of growth components, total factor productivity, capital intensity, and labor quality or labor input per hour. In turn, labor quality is decomposed into a series of main and interactive effects between characteristics of employment, in a manner analogous to the analysis of variance. This permits a detailed examination of growth and declines in labor productivity.

This chapter first hypothesizes on the long-run behavior of productivity, then details the production function approach used to construct the sources of growth measures. The data used in the application, a cross-classification of inputs in the U.S. private domestic economy for 1947–1974, and empirical results are described in the last two sections.

The sample period exhibits declining growth rates of labor productivity after the mid-1960s. Of the three components, total factor productivity declines sharply, falling to almost zero after growing at its historical rate of over 1 percent. Together with slower growth of capital intensity and labor quality over the period, the effect is to generate the productivity slowdown described in Nordhaus (1972).

The detailed disaggregation of labor inputs reveals that the contribution of educational composition to labor productivity declines by over 25 percent from 1963–1967 to 1971–1974, suggesting that the collapse of relative wages of educated workers is occurring more rapidly than the growth of their employment share. For occupation, the effect on productivity is even more deleterious. Changing occupational composition exerts a negative influence on output per hour in the 1970s, as low-wage occupations exhibit the fastest employment growth rates.

The shifting age-sex composition is analyzed for its upper-bound effect on labor productivity, determined when all wage differences are assumed to reflect marginal product differences. Even in this case, the age-sex effects remain stable into the 1970s, indicating that the reduced growth rate of labor productivity is largely unattributable to age-sex composition. Finally, workers are distinguished by class, as either employees or self-employed. Denison (1974) has documented gains in resource allocation from shifting factors from noncorporate to corporate activity. All results in this area depend on assumptions about psychic income obtained in self-employment and the imputed factor prices assigned to labor and capital. With these caveats, it is shown that the self-employment decline continues to raise output per hour, but at a slower rate.

### Hypotheses and Explanations of Productivity Growth

In his sources of growth study of the U.S., Solow (1957) obtained

$$\Delta \ln A = \Delta \ln Y - s_K \, \Delta \ln K - s_L \, \Delta \ln L$$

where $\Delta$ is the first-difference operator. The growth of total factor productivity $A$ is equal to the growth of value added $Y$, less the growth of capital $K$ weighted by its share $s_K$ and the growth of labor input $L$ weighted by its share $s_L$. With a Cobb-Douglas specification implying constancy in $s_K$ and $s_L$ the growth of total factor productivity is estimated at about 1 percent per annum for 1901–1949.

This result has remained robust to a more disaggregated form of capital and labor input specification. It is argued that if quality indices augmenting capital and labor inputs are introduced, total factor productivity growth is reduced. However, this assumes that embodied technical change in capital and labor inputs occurs at positive rates.[1]

Growth rates of about 1 percent have been obtained for total factor productivity in a series of other studies, notably those by Denison (1974) for the U.S. business sector 1929–1969 (where the growth rate is termed "advances to knowledge") and by Kendrick (1973) for the private sector 1947–1969. Alternatively, Gollop and Jorgenson (1980) formulate a sources of growth equation for gross output, determined by capital, labor, and intermediate inputs. Total factor productivity in this context is gross output per unit of gross inputs.

The above indicates a growth rate of about 1 percent for total factor productivity. A testable hypothesis is whether the historical growth rate is maintained for 1947–1974.

Capital services cannot be aggregated into a notionally homogeneous commodity such as total hours of labor. Rather, capital is measured in efficiency units of services. The results from Solow (1957) indicate that capital intensity weighted by share or $s_K \Delta \ln(K/H)$ where $H$ is total hours worked have increased secularly at $1\frac{1}{2}$ percent annually. However, subsequent events may have caused a decline in capital intensity. From the mid-1960s, the growth of employment of married women and youth has become an established phenomenon (Freeman 1977). The increase in labor supply reduces the relative wage of labor and induces labor intensity. Also, it has been demonstrated that raw material inputs, notably fuels, are relatively complementary with capital and substitutable for labor. In a perod of increasing relative prices of materials and fuels, the growth of capital intensity declines.[2] The 1960s also ushered in regulations on capital construction and formation which may have increased the relative price of capital services.

The growth of labor quality is $\Delta \ln(L/H)$, or labor services per hour worked. Given the relative constancy of the labor share over time, the change in the contribution of labor skills depends on $\Delta\ln(L/H)$. Measures of $s_L\Delta\ln(L/H)$ of about 0.6 percent per annum have been presented.[3] The periods cover 1939–1969 and the estimate is relatively stable.

By examining a disaggregated labor structure, it is possible to examine the stability of labor quality and alternative hypotheses. For each sex, labor is classified by five characteristics into various levels as follows:

> *education* (5):   elementary school or no schooling (0–8 years), 1–3 years of high school, 4 years of high school, 1–3 years of college, 4 or more years of college.
>
> *occupation* (10):   professional, managerial, farmers and farm managers, clerical, sales, crafts, operative, service (including private household workers), farm laborers, laborers.
>
> *class of worker* (2):   private wage and salary employees, self-employed and unpaid family workers.
>
> *age* (8):   14–15, 16–17, 18–24, 25–34, 35–44, 45–54, 55–64, 65 or above.

Multiplying together the numbers of levels for each characteristic (indicated in parentheses) and doubling the product (for the two sexes) yields 1,600, the total number of categories of labor. For each category, total hours worked and an hourly wage are constructed annually for 1947–1974. With the classification, it is possible to examine hypotheses on labor quality.

The observed constancy of the labor quality effect is based on a relatively fine classification of labor input. Freeman (1977, 1978) and Griliches (1977) have documented declining and overstated rates of return to higher education. However, this need not reduce the contribution of education to the growth of labor productivity. Suppose the labor aggregate is $L_t(E_{1t}, \ldots, E_{Nt}, t)$ where $E_{it}$, $i = 1, \ldots, N$ represents the hours worked by persons with educational attainment $i$ at time $t$. Wages of each group are denoted $W_{it}$, $i = 1, \ldots, N$. Under efficient labor markets

$$\partial \ln L_t/\partial t = \sum_{i=1}^{N} s_{it}\, \partial \ln E_{it}/\partial t$$

where $s_{it} \equiv \ldots W_{it}E_{it}/\Sigma_{i-1}^{N} W_{it}E_{it}$ is the compensation share of the ith labor type.

Let the $i$ index rank educational attainment in ascending order. If the relative wage of group $N$ declines with respect to all others, its absolute wage remains the greatest. Further, if group $N$ has a relatively large increase in hours worked $\partial \ln E_{Nt}/\partial t$, the contribution to labor input of the highly educated can increase. Labor quality is labor services per hour, or $\partial \ln L_t/\partial t - \partial \ln H_t/\partial t$ where $H_t = \Sigma_{i-1}^{N} E_{it}$. The sources of growth analysis will demonstrate that growth in labor quality is one of the components of growth in labor productivity. It is therefore possible to determine whether the deterioration in relative wages of the educated has reduced productivity growth. These propositions are derived more formally in a subsequent section.

Occupational structure has emerged as a positive contributor to growth in labor quality and, by extension growth, in labor productivity (Waldorf 1973). Higher-than-average growth rates in hours worked for 1952–1967 were observed in skilled occupations.[4] However, Freeman (1977) provides evidence that since 1969 the share of professional and managerial employees in the total has remained constant. If these groups also have falling relative wages, the contribution of occupation to labor quality and productivity growth is negative.

The age-sex composition of employment has shifted relatively toward youth and women since the mid-1960s. On average, women are paid lower wages than men, and younger workers are paid lower wages than older workers. Some of the differential is attributable to experience, the remainder to factors such as discrimination. A worst-case scenario for the relative growth of youth and female employment is constructed, where all wage differentials are attributable to productivity. This yields an upper bound for the decline in labor productivity.

If wage rates and returns to capital in the corporate sector are applied to factor wages in the noncorporate sector, the imputed total exceeds noncorporate income.[5] The implication is that, provided psychic income in noncorporate activity is zero, resources are more productively used if transferred to the corporate sector. The secular decline of farms and other noncorporate activity is a source of productivity growth. Whether this pattern has been maintained is a testable hypothesis.

The hypotheses are summarized in Table 4.1 for all forms of labor productivity change. The focus is on shifts within the labor market and the composition of skill. A formal structure to test the hypotheses posed remains to be derived.

## Estimation and Measurement of Labor Productivity

### Labor Productivity

Labor productivity measures are derived with respect to an underlying output or value added aggregate. This is,

$$y = df(x_1, \ldots, x_{M+1}, \ldots, x_M, x_N) \tag{4.1}$$

where $x_1, \ldots, x_M$ denotes labor inputs of different categories, indexed by such characteristics as education and experience, and $x_{M+1}, \ldots, x_N$ are nonlabor inputs. Total factor productivity or value added per unit of input $f$ is $d$. The aggregate function satisfies the conditions, where $x = (x_1, \ldots, x_N)$ of:

   i.   monotonicity: $f(x)$ increasing for $x_i$ increasing,
       $x_i \geq O, i = l, \ldots, N$
   ii.  linear homogeneity: $f(\lambda x) = \lambda f(x), \lambda \geq 0$
   iii. concavity: $f(\lambda x^1 + (1 - \lambda)x^2) \geq \lambda f(x^1) + (1 - \lambda)f(x^2)$,
       $0 \leq \lambda < 1, x^1 \geqq 0, x^2 \geqq 0. \tag{4.2}$

The labor inputs are measured in hours worked and represented by the subaggregate $z(x_1, \ldots, x_M)$. Analogously, capital is the subaggregate $k(x_{M+1}, \ldots, x_N)$. Provided that the labor and capital subaggregates also satisfy conditions (4.2), little information is lost by forming these groupings.[6]

An alternative method of measuring labor input is by summation of hours worked over categories, yielding total hours $h = \Sigma_{i=1}^M x_i$. Hence, labor input can be expressed

$$z = z(x_1, \ldots, x_M)$$
$$= hz(x_1/h, \ldots, x_M/h)$$
$$= hq(x_1, \ldots, x_M) \tag{4.3}$$

where $q(x_1, \ldots, x_M)$ is the index of labor quality provided per hour worked, or $z/h$. Only if all hours worked in the economy are homogeneous, and consequently have identical marginal products,

**Table 4.1.**  Hypotheses of Productivity Performance (annual growth rates), U.S. Private Sector, 1947–1974

| Component | | Hypothesis |
|---|---|---|
| 1. | Labor productivity (value added per hour worked). | i. Maintaining "historical" growth of 2–3% |
| | | ii. Productivity crisis—decline to below 1% (Nordhaus 1972). |
| 2.a. | Total factor productivity (value added per unit of input index). | i. Maintaining outward shift of 1% as verified by Solow (1957).[a] |
| | | ii. Disappearance to negligible effect because of aggregation error (Jorgenson and Griliches 1967). |
| b. | Capital intensity (capital services in efficiency units per hour worked). | i. Maintaining secular growth effect of $1\frac{1}{2}\%$ (Solow 1957). |
| | | ii. Decreasing in growth because of age-sex composition of employment, fuel-capital complementarity, capital regulation. |
| c. | Labor quality (labor services in efficiency units per hour worked). | i. Maintaining secular growth rate of 0.6% (Griliches 1970). |
| | | ii. Decreasing labor quality effects: education, occupation Collapse of market for skills (Freeman 1977). Age-sex composition (growth of youth and female employment in 1960s). |

[a]Hulten (1975) has argued for even greater total factor productivity growth of over 2%, viewing produced means of production as a component.

does the index $q(x_1, \ldots, x_M) = 1$. Labor quality includes the effects of average educational attainment and other characteristics in augmenting the average hour worked.

For the capital subaggregate $d(x_{M+1}, \ldots, x_N)$ there is no analogue of total hours worked. No superficially homogeneous aggregate such as "total machines" can be used to combine the services of the nonhuman inputs. Value added is

$$y = df(qh, k) \tag{4.4}$$

under the aggregation restrictions, so differentiating with respect to time $t$ yields in equilibrium

$$\frac{\partial \ln y}{\partial t} = \frac{\partial \ln d}{\partial t} + s_z \left[ \frac{\partial \ln q}{\partial t} + \frac{\partial \ln h}{\partial t} \right] + s_k \frac{\partial \ln k}{\partial t} \tag{4.5}$$

where $s_z = \partial \ln f / \partial \ln z$ is the share of labor inputs in factor compensation and $s_k = 1 - s_z$.

Growth in value added $\partial \ln y / \partial t$ is the sum of four components, namely:

1.  total factor productivity $\partial \ln d / \partial t$, the growth in output per unit of input;
2.  labor quality $s_z \, \partial \ln q / \partial t$, the growth in the average services provided per hour, depending on skills and employment composition, weighted by the labor share;
3.  total hours worked $s_z \, \partial \ln h / \partial t$, the growth in total hours worked, regardless of skill composition, weighted by the share of labor in total compensation of factors; and
4.  capital $s_k \, \partial \ln k / \partial t$, the growth of efficiency units of capital services used weighted by the share of nonlabor inputs.

The definition of labor productivity in the national accounts is value added per hour worked.[7] Rearranging the relation for the growth in value added,

$$\frac{\partial \ln (y/h)}{\partial t} = \frac{\partial \ln d}{\partial t} + s_z \frac{\partial \ln q}{\partial t} + s_k \frac{\partial \ln (k/h)}{\partial t} \tag{4.6}$$

is the growth in labor productivity. It is also possible to derive a corresponding real wage growth function dual to the labor productivity relation. This commences with aggregation on factor prices in the cost function.[8] This is the sum of growth rates in total factor productivity and the share-weighted growth of labor quality, plus the growth of capital intensity $k/h$, weighted by the capital share. The derivation of measures underlying (4.6) is the principal objective.

Capital is measured in efficiency units and a subaggregate, and so capital intensity is a single number. Total factor productivity $d$ is $y/f$ and also a single number. However, the labor quality index $q = z/h$ depends on various characteristics of employment, and it is possible to derive a nested sources of growth relation for labor quality, expressing $\partial \ln q/\partial t$ as a function of various characteristics of labor input.

### Quality and Labor Characteristics

In the limit, the M types of labor describe precisely each hour worked in the economy, with a price $p_m$, $m = 1, \ldots, M$ for each. Practically, data restrictions and computational constraints imply that the labor subaggregate contains a limited number of characteristics $k = 1, \ldots, K$ classified into levels $i_k = 1_k, \ldots, I_k$ for the kth characteristic. Labor subaggregates have been formed with unionization as the single identifying characteristic (Brown and Medoff 1978), education (Dougherty 1972 and Bowles 1970), age (Freeman 1978 and Chinloy 1980b), occupation (Berndt and Christensen 1974) and sex (Medoff 1978).

Several characteristics may be of relevance in describing labor input as opposed to a single characteristic. For the $k$ characteristics, total hours for the $M$ labor types $x_1, \ldots, x_M$ are described as follows. If one hour worked in the economy is provided by a person with characteristics $i_1, \ldots, i_k$ then

$$\left. \begin{array}{l} x_i = x(i_1, \ldots, i_k) = 1 \\ \qquad\qquad = 0 \ \text{otherwise} \end{array} \right\} i = 1, \ldots, M \qquad (4.7)$$

and if $p(i_1, \ldots, i_k)$ is the wage for such an hour,

$$\begin{array}{l} p(i_1, \ldots, i_k) \times (i_1, \ldots, i_k) = p(i_1, \ldots, i_k) \\ \qquad\qquad\qquad = 0 \ \text{otherwise} \end{array} \qquad (4.8)$$

is the labor compensation received. For the labor subaggregate, $z(x_1, \ldots, x_M)$ can be expressed in terms of (4.7) for all $x_i$, $i = 1, \ldots, M$, with each entry represented by the characteristic levels $i_1, \ldots, i_k$. In this mutually exclusive and exhaustive classification

$$M = \prod_{k=1}^{k} I_k$$

is the number of types of labor.

As an example, suppose there are only two characteristics describing the productivity of a worker, education and age. Factor 1, education, has three levels, $I_1 = 3$, which are elementary, secondary, and postsecondary. Factor 2, age, has two levels, $I_2 = 3$, which are below 25 years of age and 25 and above. So

$$M = \prod_{k=1}^{2} I_k$$

or six and an hour worked by an elementary-educated, under-25 worker is $x(1, 2) = 1$, and $x(i_1, i_2) = 0$ for $i_1 \neq 1, i_2 \neq 2$.

In the $k$ characteristics classification, suppose all information on $i_1$, ..., $i_k$ is suppressed, and all hours worked assumed homogeneous. Then

$$h = \sum_{i=1}^{M} x_i = \sum_{i_1=1}^{I_1} \cdots \sum_{i_k=1}^{I_k} x(i_1, \ldots, i_k) \tag{4.9}$$

is total hours worked. Also

$$q(1, \ldots, k) = z(1, \ldots, k)/h \tag{4.10}$$

where $q(1, \ldots, k)$ is the labor quality index obtained when all $k$ characteristics are used in describing each hour worked, and $z(1, \ldots, k)$ is the analogous labor input index whose typical element is $x(i_1, \ldots, i_k)$. It is possible to construct main effects attributable to various characteristics. Suppose information on all characteristics save the first is suppressed. Labor is classified by levels $i_1, \ldots, I_1$ but is homogeneous within $i_1$. If education is the first characteristic, labor input is $z(1)$, dependent only on levels of schooling achieved, and labor quality is

$$q(1) = z(1)/h \tag{4.11}$$

where $z(1)$ contains typical element $x(i_1)$, $i_1 = 1, \ldots, I_1$. This conforms identically to specifications of labor input in Dougherty

(1972) and Griliches (1970) by education. The wage paid per hour for each education group is obtained by

$$p(i_1) = C(i_1)/x(i_1) \quad i_1 = 1, \ldots, I_1 \tag{4.12}$$

where

$$C(i_1) = \sum_{i_2=1}^{I_2} \cdots \sum_{i_k=1}^{I_k} p(i_1, \ldots, i_k)x(i_1, \ldots, i_k)$$

is total compensation paid to each educational level.

The measure $q(1)$ is defined as the main effect of factor 1, exemplified by education. By cycling over the characteristics, there are $k$ main effects of form $q(k)$, $k = 1, \ldots, k$. If workers are identified by education, age, sex, class, and occupation, there are five main effects.

In a complete cross-classification it is possible to identify a high school graduate, aged 25–34 years, who is male and a self-employed crafts worker. In turn, interactions between the characteristics are computable. Suppose labor is classified by the first two characteristics, education and age. Instead of $M = I$, as in (4.11), there are $I_1 I_2$ types of labor, and

$$q(1, 2) = z(1, 2)/h \tag{4.13}$$

where workers are homogeneous in each education-age level, so

$$x(i_1, i_2) = \sum_{i_3=1}^{I_3} \cdots \sum_{i_k=1}^{I_k} x(i_1, \ldots, i_k),$$

and information on the remaining $(k - 2)$ characteristics is suppressed. The wage for each of these $I_1 I_2$ labor types is

$$p(i_1, i_2) = C(i_1, i_2)/x(i_1, i_2) \tag{4.14}$$

where

$$C(i_1, i_2) = \sum_{i_3=1}^{I_3} \cdots \sum_{i_k=1}^{I_k} p(i_3, \ldots, i_k)x(i_3, \ldots, i_k)$$

is total compensation paid in each education-age group. If there are $k$ characteristics, by cycling there are $k(k - 1)/2$ indices containing two factors, as in (4.13). By induction, the process of suppressing the characteristics can be extended from the two-factor to the $(k - 1)$ factor case. There is one $k$ factor labor quality index (4.10). The objective is to use these partial information indices to construct measures of quality effects for various characteristics.[9]

For the two-factor education-age case, $q(1, 2)$ represents labor quality when hours are classified by both characteristics, while $q(1)$ and $q(2)$ are the respective education and age quality indices. Then

$$b(1, 2) = q(1, 2)/q(1)q(2) \tag{4.15}$$

is the first-order interactive effect between the factors, or in logarithms

$$\ln b(1, 2) = \ln z(1, 2) - h - (\ln z(1) - h) - \ln z(2) - h)$$

$$= \ln z(1, 2) - \ln z(1) - \ln z(2) + h \tag{4.16}$$

is the first-order interaction between the first two factors. By analogy with the analysis of variance, interactions of all orders up to $(N - 1)$ can be constructed from a classification by $N$ characteristics.

In the two-factor case, the labor quality index is, in logarithms

$$\ln q(1, 2) = \ln q(1) + \ln q(2) + \ln b(1, 2) \tag{4.17}$$

and its $N$ factor analogue is the sum of a series of main and interactive effects. For $N$ factors, there are $N$ main effects, $N(N - 1)/2$ first-order interactions, and in general $[N(N - 1) \ldots (N - k)]/k!$ entries of order $(k - 1)$. In the five-factor classification of labor input used, there are five main effects for education, occupation, age, sex, and class. Using the notation $E$, $J$, $A$, $S$, and $C$ to represent the five factors, the interactions are:

first order (10):  $b(E, J)$, $b(E, A)$, $b(E, S)$, $b(E, C)$, $b(J, A)$, $b(J, S)$, $b(J, C)$, $b(A, S)$, $b(A, C)$, $b(S, C)$.

second order (10):  $b(E, J, A)$, $b(E, J, S)$, $b(E, J, C)$, $b(E, A, S)$, $b(E, A, C)$, $b(E, S, C)$, $b(J, A, S)$, $b(J, S, C)$, $b(A, S, C)$.

third order (5):  $b(E, J, A, S)$, $b(E, J, A, C)$, $b(E, J, S, C)$, $b(E, A, S, C)$, $b(J, A, S, C)$.

fourth order (1):  $b(E, J, A, S, C)$.

The number of interactions is indicated in parentheses. The product of these twenty-six interactions and the five main effects $q(E)$, $q(J)$, $q(A)$, $q(S)$, and $q(C)$ is equal to the five-factor labor quality index

$$q(E, J, A, S, C) = z(E, J, A, S, C)/h. \tag{4.18}$$

The labor input index $z(E, J, A, S, C,)$ is constructed for the full five-factor classification into all levels, or 1,600 groups of labor.

To perform the complete methodology, total factor productivity estimates are constructed using (4.5) where $\partial \ln d/\partial t$ is the residual or balancing item. The sources of labor productivity relation (4.6) is constructed, and this is decomposed for the labor quality components. The labor quality effect is $s_z \partial \ln q(E, J, A, S, C)/\partial t$. The contribution of each labor component to total labor productivity growth is

$$a(i) = s_z \partial \ln q(i)/\partial t \qquad i = E, J, A, S, C. \tag{4.19}$$

### Data Construction

The data on labor input are the same as those described in Chapters 2 and 3. However, for total factor productivity it is necessary also to construct data on capital.

For the capital data, total capital income is value added in current dollars less labor compensation, using series from the BEA, by industry. From the reported investment series and a capital stock benchmark, series on capital stocks are constructed by the perpetual inventory method.[10] This series $k_t$, $t = 1947, \ldots, 1974$ is divided into total capital income to yield the rate of return on capital. The calculation is

$$r_t = (P_t VA_t - \sum_{i=1}^{1600} w_{i,t} h_{i,t})/k_t \tag{4.20}$$

where $r_t$ is the rate of return, $P_t$ is the price index for value added, and $VA_t$ is the constant dollar value added. The series on the price deflator for business output reported by the BEA is used for $P_t$. Capital income is $r_t k_t$ and the share of capital is $s_k = r_t k_t/P_t VA_t$.

### Specification and Empirical Results

Empirical implementation requires a specification of the technology of production. Diewert (1978) and Allen and Diewert

(1981) have shown that, provided superlative index number forms are used, the error in comparing alternative specifications is negligible. Superlative index numbers are associated with forms providing second-order approximations to the underlying production function.

A translog form is selected to approximate the production function. Since this form is approximately consistent in aggregation, the results are robust to whether an index of value added can be constructed as separable from raw material and intermediate inputs (Diewart 1978).[11]

The first procedure is to construct estimates for the growth rate of total factor productivity, specifying (4.5). For the translog form

$$\Delta \ln d_t = \Delta \ln y_t - v_{zt}[\Delta \ln q_t + \Delta \ln h_t] - v_{kt}\Delta \ln k_t \quad (4.21)$$

where $\Delta$ is the first difference operator and $v_{zt} = (s_{z,t} + s_{z,t+1})/2$ is the aggregate labor share and $v_{kt} = 1 - v_{zt}$ obtains in discrete time (Diewert 1976). The next procedure, corresponding to (4.6), is to form the sources of labor productivity growth relation

$$\Delta \ln (y_t/h_t) = \Delta \ln d_t + v_{zt} \Delta \ln q_t + v_{kt} \Delta \ln (k_t/h_t). \quad (4.22)$$

For the decomposition of labor skills, translog forms are specified for all partial subaggregates. The one-factor index growth rate in (4.11) is $\Delta \ln z(1)$, with components $\Delta \ln x(1), \ldots, \Delta \ln x(I_1)$. The form, which uses a moving average compensation share $v(i_1)$ over adjacent time periods as weights, yields

$$\Delta \ln q(1) = \sum_{i_1-1}^{I_1} v(i_1) \Delta \ln x(i_1) - \Delta \ln h \quad (4.23)$$

as the main effect and

$$a(1) = v_z \Delta \ln q(1) \quad (4.24)$$

as the contribution to productivity growth for any time period $t$. Interactive effects are constructed using translog specifications for all $\Delta \ln z$ aggregates, or share weighting with moving averages on included subsets of characteristics. The contribution of labor input growth $v_{zt} \Delta \ln q_t$ is ultimately decomposed into a series of main and interactive effects, as described in section 2b, with the relevant $z$ index specified to be translog.[12]

The results on estimation of total factor productivity growth are

reported in Table 4.2. Total factor productivity grows at the historically consistent rate of 1.178 percent per annum for 1947–1967.
These estimates appear to support the long-term rates of slightly
greater than 1 percent obtained by Solow (1957) for 1901–1949.
However, for the period 1967–1974 total factor productivity almost
disappears, supporting the Jorgenson-Griliches (1967, 1972) hypothesis that under fine disaggregation of inputs such growth is zero. From
1967 to 1974, total factor productivity grows at 0.078 percent per
annum. The results indicate a substantial deterioration in output per
unit of inputs. While the average growth rate of total factor productivity is 0.899 percent annually, this rate is not maintained in the last
part of the sample period.

Over the 1947–1974 period, total factor productivity accounts for
25.8 percent of the growth in value added (a conclusion obtained by
dividing the average of column (1) by that of column (2) of Table
4.2). The labor effect $v_z \Delta \ln z$ averages 0.913 percent annually, and
accounts for 26.2 percent of value-added growth, while the capital
effect $v_k \Delta \ln k$ is 1.671 percent and accounts for 48.0 percent.
However, in the 1967–1974 period, total factor productivity accounts
for only 2.8 percent of the growth in value added. This further
indicates the disappearance or nonexistence of total factor productivity.

In addition, the functional distribution of income, found constant
by Solow (1957), shifts in favor of capital and against labor during the
1947–1974 period. The share of labor compensation in payments in
the private domestic economy is 63.2 percent in 1947–1951, and this
declines monotonically to 58.7 percent in 1963–1967, although a
small increase occurs after this period. Since capital services increase
more rapidly than labor services during the period, an additional
fillip to output growth is provided by the rising capital share.

Table 4.3 indicates the labor productivity decomposition. Growth
in output per hour worked is the sum of total factor productivity, a
labor quality effect, and a capital intensity effect, in growth form.
Labor productivity grows at 2.614 percent from 1947 to 1974, but
declines to a 0.649 percent growth rate from 1971 to 1974. The results
confirm the productivity slowdown discussed in Nordhaus (1972). In
the 1947–1955 period, output per hour increased at over 3.5 percent
per annum, but in the 1960s and thereafter the growth rate dropped
to less than half of this.

**Table 4.2.** Total Factor Productivity, Value Added, Labor, and Capital Input Growth Rates, U.S. Private Sector, 1947–1974 (average percent per year)

| | (1) | (2) | (3) | (4) | (5) | (6) | (7) |
|---|---|---|---|---|---|---|---|
| | Total Factor Productivity $\Delta\ln d$ | Value Added $\Delta\ln y$ | Labor Share (compensation) $v_z$ | Labor Input $\Delta\ln z$ | Capital Share (compensation) $v_k = 1 - v_z$ | Capital Input $\Delta\ln k$ | Hours Worked $\Delta\ln h$ |
| 1947–1951 | 0.950 | 4.249 | 0.632 | 1.730 | 0.368 | 5.994 | 0.592 |
| 1951–1955 | 1.515 | 3.742 | 0.621 | 1.121 | 0.379 | 4.038 | 0.292 |
| 1955–1959 | 0.161 | 2.087 | 0.622 | 0.882 | 0.378 | 3.645 | 0.287 |
| 1959–1963 | 1.407 | 3.622 | 0.607 | 1.501 | 0.393 | 3.319 | 0.251 |
| 1963–1967 | 1.860 | 5.230 | 0.587 | 2.306 | 0.413 | 4.806 | 2.539 |
| 1967–1971 | 0.234 | 2.400 | 0.599 | 0.823 | 0.401 | 4.172 | 0.264 |
| 1971–1974 | −0.128 | 3.210 | 0.597 | 2.677 | 0.403 | 4.293 | 2.552 |
| 1947–1974 | 0.899 | 3.483 | 0.610 | 1.496 | 0.390 | 4.285 | 0.869 |

**Table 4.3.** Sources of Growth in Labor Productivity, U.S. Private Sector, 1947–1974 (average percent per year)

|  | (1) Labor Productivity $\Delta\ln(y/h)$ | (2) Total Factor Productivity $\Delta\ln d$ | (3) Labor Quality Effect $v_z\Delta\ln(z/h)$ | (4) Capital Intensity Effect $v_k\Delta\ln(k/h)$ |
|---|---|---|---|---|
| 1947–1951 | 3.657 | 0.950 | 0.720 | 1.987 |
| 1951–1955 | 3.449 | 1.515 | 0.515 | 1.419 |
| 1955–1959 | 1.799 | 0.161 | 0.370 | 1.268 |
| 1959–1963 | 3.370 | 1.407 | 0.759 | 1.204 |
| 1963–1967 | 2.658 | 1.860 | −0.137 | 0.935 |
| 1967–1971 | 2.134 | 0.234 | 0.335 | 1.565 |
| 1971–1974 | 0.649 | −0.128 | 0.075 | 0.702 |
| *1947–1974* | *2.614* | *0.899* | *0.383* | *1.332* |

Total factor productivity, in its decline from 1967 to 1974, is shown to be a major contributor to the slowdown. From 1947 to 1963, labor productivity increased at 3.06 percent annually and total factor productivity at 1.01 percent, or 33.0 percent of the total. From 1967 to 1974, labor productivity increased at 1.50 percent, and total factor productivity accounted for 5.2 percent of the total. Consequently, the decline in output per unit of input is associated with the decline in labor productivity.

The labor quality effect is $v_z\Delta\ln(z/h)$, labor quality multiplied by the labor share. This component also exhibits a decline, with the turning point occurring earlier than for labor productivity, in 1963–1967. From 1947 to 1963 the labor quality effect increased at 0.590 percent annually, but from 1963 to 1974 the effect declines to 0.092 percent, virtually disappearing. As a proportion of the total, labor quality accounts for 6.1 percent of labor productivity growth for 1947–1963 and 4.8 percent for 1963–1974. A decline in labor services per hour also emerges as a major contributor to the productivity slowdown. In the last decade of the sample, there is virtually no increase in total factor productivity or labor quality, and the disappearance of these effects reduces output per hour.

Capital intensity has an effect of $v_k\Delta \ln (k/h)$, capital services in efficiency units per hour worked weighted by the capital share. Over the 1947–1963 period, this deepening of capital contributed 1.47 percent annually to labor productivity growth, or 48.0 percent of the total, making this the largest single contributor. For 1963–1974 capital intensity effects contribute 1.10 percent annually. However, about 90 percent of the growth in labor productivity observed during the period arises from capital intensity. The results indicate a reduction in capital intensity growth, but that the labor productivity slowdown is attributable to declines in the remaining two components.

Total factor productivity is a single index, but labor quality can be decomposed into a series of effects associated with the characteristics of sex, age, class, occupation, and education. The sum of these effects is $v_z\Delta \ln (z/h)$. The results are indicated in Table 4.4.

The first block indicates the main effect of each characteristic in labor productivity growth. Each is based on a translog labor subaggregate dependent only on the levels of the characteristic considered. The first row, first column entry indicates a negative contribution of sex composition to labor productivity of 0.09 percent annually for 1947–1974. This is based on a labor subaggregate $z(S_{1t}, S_{2t})$ where $S_1$ and $S_2$ are hours worked of men and women. If $z$ is translog, the productivity effect is

$$a_t(S) = v_{zt}[v_{1t}\Delta \ln S_{1t} + v_{2t}\Delta \ln S_{2t} - \Delta \ln h]$$

where $v_{1t}$, $i = 1, 2$ are moving average weights of labor compensation shares by sex.

Throughout, education emerges as the largest main effect, increasing labor productivity by 0.383 percent in 1947–1974 and accounting for 14 percent of this increase. The education effect, reading across the E row, increases monotonically from 0.17 percent in 1947–1951 to 0.50 percent 1963–1967, but declines thereafter. For 1971–1974 the education effect is 0.40 percent, a decline of 25 percent from the peak. The declining relative wages of the educated dampen their increasing employment share. It is apparent that the collapse of the education market in this period spills over into productivity reductions. Nevertheless, the productivity slowdown is not principally attributable to education. In fact, given that labor productivity as a whole increases at only 0.649 percent in 1971–1974, the education effect alone accounts for almost two-thirds of the entire growth.

The deteriorating condition of the labor market for skilled workers is more evident in the occupational data. In the 1947–1974 period, the contribution of shifting job distribution towards those with above-average wages increases labor productivity by 0.19 percent per year. However, after 1963 this effect becomes negligible, and is negative for 1971–1974. The occupation main effect accounts for 7.29 percent of total labor productivity growth over the period, and for 1963–1974 the average occupational effect is 0.1 percent per annum. Freeman (1977) has presented evidence on the declining market for people in skilled occupations after 1969. It is shown that the share of professional and managerial jobs in the total has remained constant and relative wages of these groups has declined. The observed results support a decline in the effect of changing skill composition on labor productivity. They also suggest that little gain in labor productivity is attainable through inducing a shift in occupational composition, for example, by investing in training.

The effect of class, measuring the shift from self-employment to employee status, is not independent of the imputation procedure for pricing noncorporate capital and labor inputs. Christensen (1971) assigns average compensation of employees to the self-employed, and any quality effects arise in capital inputs.[13] Such a procedure implies a zero class effect on labor inputs. Denison (1974) uses a hybrid, assigning part of the noncorporate income shortfall to both labor and capital.

The procedure used for the results in Table 4.4, row 2, assigns all the lower noncorporate factor income to labor, following the Kuznets (1971) approach. As in other procedures, psychic income in the noncorporate sector is assumed to be zero. These assumptions result in an upper-bound estimate of the effect of class on labor productivity. Nevertheless, the effect is small, particularly after 1963, where the annual average effect is 0.03 percent. The results suggest that little productivity gain can be made by reallocating labor from noncorporate to corporate activity, even under assumptions favorable to such a conclusion.

The effect of sex composition is negative throughout the period. However, this is the largest negative effect on productivity that is assignable, for it is assumed that none of the male-female wage

**Table 4.4.** Labor Skill Contributions to Labor Productivity Growth, U.S. Private Domestic Economy, 1947–1974

| | 1947–1974 | 1947–1951 | 1951–1955 | 1955–1959 | 1959–1963 | 1963–1967 | 1967–1971 | 1971–1974 |
|---|---|---|---|---|---|---|---|---|
| **Main effects** | | | | | | | | |
| S | -0.094 | 0.024 | -0.116 | -0.211 | -0.030 | -0.140 | -0.132 | -0.035 |
| C | 0.088 | 0.176 | 0.082 | 0.160 | 0.087 | 0.025 | 0.032 | 0.054 |
| A | -0.005 | 0.217 | 0.168 | 0.021 | -0.039 | -0.130 | -0.122 | -0.174 |
| E | 0.383 | 0.171 | 0.313 | 0.364 | 0.436 | 0.500 | 0.483 | 0.399 |
| J | 0.198 | 0.398 | 0.196 | 0.260 | 0.224 | 0.085 | 0.240 | -0.064 |
| | 0.570 | 0.986 | 0.643 | 0.594 | 0.678 | 0.340 | 0.501 | 0.180 |
| **Interactive Effects** | | | | | | | | |
| *First Order* | | | | | | | | |
| SC | 0.034 | 0.034 | -0.001 | 0.006 | 0.083 | 0.098 | -0.001 | 0.011 |
| SA | 0.013 | -0.042 | -0.014 | -0.017 | 0.076 | 0.072 | 0.010 | -0.005 |
| SE | 0.043 | 0.016 | 0.035 | 0.057 | 0.080 | 0.075 | 0.018 | 0.009 |
| SJ | 0.059 | -0.005 | 0.073 | 0.108 | 0.103 | 0.087 | 0.041 | -0.015 |
| CA | 0.026 | 0.044 | 0.035 | 0.015 | 0.072 | 0.025 | -0.005 | -0.017 |
| CE | -0.029 | -0.016 | -0.027 | -0.034 | 0.035 | -0.115 | -0.021 | -0.014 |
| CJ | -0.006 | -0.061 | -0.039 | -0.077 | 0.043 | -0.301 | 0.019 | -0.027 |
| AE | 0.013 | 0.008 | 0.030 | -0.001 | 0.074 | 0.018 | -0.007 | -0.041 |
| AJ | -0.001 | -0.066 | -0.026 | -0.024 | 0.053 | -0.001 | 0.024 | 0.035 |
| EJ | -0.168 | -0.137 | -0.189 | -0.256 | -0.107 | -0.210 | -0.212 | -0.028 |
| | -0.076 | -0.225 | -0.123 | -0.223 | 0.512 | -0.252 | -0.134 | -0.092 |

| | | | | | | | | |
|---|---|---|---|---|---|---|---|---|
| **Second Order** | | | | | | | | |
| SCA | −0.018 | −0.009 | −0.006 | −0.006 | −0.055 | −0.039 | 0.000 | −0.004 |
| SCE | −0.019 | −0.003 | 0.005 | 0.002 | −0.061 | −0.062 | −0.002 | −0.004 |
| SCJ | −0.038 | −0.039 | −0.001 | −0.006 | −0.092 | −0.118 | 0.005 | −0.008 |
| SAE | −0.012 | −0.008 | −0.014 | −0.012 | −0.057 | 0.000 | 0.012 | 0.003 |
| SAJ | −0.015 | 0.014 | −0.007 | −0.005 | −0.056 | −0.043 | 0.001 | −0.005 |
| SEJ | −0.045 | −0.021 | −0.020 | −0.037 | −0.100 | −0.073 | −0.030 | −0.021 |
| CAE | 0.002 | 0.008 | 0.017 | 0.017 | −0.038 | −0.011 | 0.013 | 0.010 |
| CAJ | −0.020 | −0.027 | −0.020 | −0.012 | −0.067 | −0.002 | −0.007 | 0.003 |
| CEJ | 0.004 | 0.015 | 0.024 | 0.029 | −0.050 | 0.025 | −0.007 | −0.014 |
| AEJ | −0.005 | 0.015 | 0.018 | 0.034 | −0.075 | −0.029 | −0.008 | 0.014 |
| | −0.166 | −0.055 | 0.004 | 0.004 | −0.651 | −0.352 | −0.023 | −0.026 |
| **Third Order** | | | | | | | | |
| SCAE | 0.013 | 0.005 | −0.001 | 0.000 | 0.067 | 0.017 | 0.000 | 0.002 |
| SCAJ | 0.015 | 0.007 | 0.004 | 0.004 | 0.059 | 0.024 | −0.002 | 0.004 |
| SCEJ | 0.021 | 0.003 | −0.003 | 0.001 | 0.061 | 0.077 | 0.002 | 0.002 |
| SAEJ | 0.016 | 0.008 | 0.010 | 0.010 | 0.061 | 0.016 | −0.004 | 0.006 |
| CAEJ | 0.004 | −0.004 | −0.014 | −0.015 | 0.043 | 0.018 | −0.002 | 0.001 |
| | 0.069 | 0.019 | −0.004 | 0.000 | 0.291 | 0.152 | −0.006 | 0.015 |
| **Fourth Order** | | | | | | | | |
| SCAEJ | −0.015 | −0.005 | 0.000 | 0.000 | −0.068 | −0.020 | −0.002 | −0.002 |
| *Quality Change* | 0.383 | 0.720 | 0.520 | 0.375 | 0.762 | −0.132 | 0.336 | 0.075 |

(S) SEX,   (C) CLASS,   (A) AGE,   (E) EDUCATION,   (J) OCCUPATION

differential arises through discrimination.[14] The sex effect reduces labor productivity by 0.09 percent per year, or about 7 percent over the entire period. Moreover, the point estimate for the effect declined to 0.04 percent for 1971–1974. A maximal decline in labor productivity amounting to less than one-tenth of 1 percent per annum in a period where the average grew by 2.61 percent is not substantial. Moreover, the sex effect remains relatively constant through the 1960s, when the productivity slowdown commenced. This implies that the slowdown is not principally attributable to the rapid employment of female workers with respect to males.

The age effect reverses sign after 1959 and is associated with the slowdown. Age composition raises output per hour by 0.22 percent for 1947–1951 and reduces it by 0.17 percent for 1971–1974. If the age effect were at its 1947–1974 average of −0.01 percent, labor productivity growth would have been 25 percent greater in 1971–1974. Clearly, the rapid relative employment of inexperienced youth is reducing labor productivity. These conclusions are vitiated by two considerations. First, there may be wage distortions in the data that act against youth, such as discrimination or lower relative presence in unions or jobs with specific skills. Second, youth may be trading off current wages for improved training opportunities that will steepen their wage profiles. The latter suggests the possibility of a reversal of the age effect as the average age of employment increases.

The interactive effects in sum reduce the growth of labor productivity, implying that the main effects exaggerate the contribution of skills. This is particularly evident in the first-order education-occupation interaction, which averages −0.16 percent and thus is almost as large as the occupation effect. If education and occupation are measuring the same variable—skill—then the interaction eliminates one of these characteristics. The conclusion is that education and occupation together contribute a total of 0.40 percent to labor productivity for 1947–1974, not the 0.56 percent suggested by main effects only.

## Concluding Remarks

In the structure presented, total factor productivity is a single number, being the ratio of output to an input index. It is shown that the decline in total factor productivity is an important contributor to the decline in U.S. labor productivity. The focus is on the labor market and on how changes in employment composition affect how much is produced per hour.

In principle, there is no reason why capital cannot similarly be disaggregated. Examples of characteristics are industry of use, type of capital (residential or nonresidential structures, land, equipment, and inventory), and legal form of organization (corporate or noncorporate). The problem is that, since there is no "homogeneous" unit of capital analogous to an hour worked, the constructed capital index must always be expressed in efficiency units. Further, it is not possible to construct measures of quality in a corresponding manner, given the absence of "homogeneous" capital.

The sources of growth analysis attempts to be more causal in explanation, although this is not completely the case. The usual methodology expresses output growth as dependent upon input growth, in an appropriate weighting scheme. However, input growth is not exogenous and may not explain output growth so much as occur simultaneously with it. By taking the step backward to the labor market and its composition, it may be possible to adopt a more causal explanation for productivity change.

Some of the results need not be robust for assumptions to be made. If people obtain psychic benefits from being their own employers, the class effect is reduced. If women are discriminated against, the negative sex effect is reduced. These characteristics do not have a substantial effect on labor productivity, but the results may differ if wage differentials unrelated to measured marginal product are introduced. There may be selectivity bias (Gronau 1974) in that the actual job opportunities facing people are less favorable than those observed, because reservation wages vary with characteristics and truncate out lower-wage jobs. Selectivity bias affects all studies where market wage data are used.

Apart from these issues raised, the *CPS* survey week may not be representative of the year, and underreporting of high earnings may artificially compress relative wage distributions. Also, for years with scant information on detailed cross-classifications, it is necessary to use the biproportional procedure, which implies low substitution possibilities between workers. Among the characteristics used, age (Freeman 1978), sex (Medoff 1978), and education (Tinbergen 1975) appear to exhibit this property, but further research is needed.

# 5

# AGGREGATION OF INPUTS AND TECHNICAL CHANGE

The conventional approach to the estimation of production functions involves the use of the aggregate inputs of capital and labor. These composites represent respectively indices of nonhuman and human services utilized in production. Alternative methods of constructing binary mutually exclusive and exhaustive indices of factor inputs involve aggregation into process and overhead services and into skilled and unskilled services. Process or productive inputs include various categories of blue-collar or production labor, raw materials and intermediate inputs, energy and fuel, and machine services utilized. Overhead inputs include white-collar or nonproduction labor categories and the services of land and structures. Given that utilization rates are more directly controllable for production than nonproduction inputs, these can respectively be interpreted as variable and fixed factors in production.

By analogy with the theory of consumer behavior, where a listing of inputs can be truncated to a listing of needs, production can be assumed to take place with a group of skills.[1] All inputs in the original listing can be expressed as linear combinations of the group of skills. A skill can be defined as an index of perfectly substitutable or perfectly complementary inputs. Consequently, a skill can be interpreted to represent any form of factor composite, including capital and labor and production and nonproduction indices. For these purposes, the definition of skill is specialized to include white-collar labor inputs and all nonhuman factors with which such factors can be aggregated. Analogously, an unskilled input is defined to include unskilled labor

74

inputs and nonhuman factors of production aggregable with these inputs.

Technical change, if factor augmenting, acts to increase the efficiency level of each factor of production. If the rates of augmentation are equal for a group of factors, an index can be constructed augmenting all factors in the group. In particular, tests of equality of all augmentation rates for factors in a given group can be performed. A restrictive form of such change is the Hicks augmenting case where all rates are equal.

Tests for the binary composites of labor and capital, production and nonproduction, skilled and unskilled are detailed for a classification containing equipment, plant, blue-collar workers, and white-collar workers. Such aggregates for homothetic production imply that the elasticities of substitution between any factor within a grouping and a given factor outside the grouping be equal. From the associated elasticities, hypotheses on production can be tested, particularly complementarity between capital and skilled labor and substitutability between labor and equipment.

The considered groupings are tested for pairwise equality of rates of augmentation, given factor augmentation, which is tested prior to these hypotheses. A production specification is derived for the input and technology aggregates, and empirical results presented for the United States private domestic economy for 1948–1972. The principal conclusions are that separable aggregates of production or variable and nonproduction or fixed inputs exist, satisfying the regularity conditions of the two-level constant elasticity of substitution (CES) form. In addition, technical change can be indexed by the same augmentation rate for all factors.

## Production Specification

Production is assumed to take place with a function expressing output as an aggregate of the services of equipment, plant, blue-collar and white-collar workers, and time. A translog approximation to this function is specified, and the regularity conditions of monotonicity and convexity are parametrized. Test procedures for hypothesis on technical change and aggregation are subsequently developed.

The underlying production function is

$$Y = F(X_1, X_2, X_3, X_4, t) \qquad (5.1)$$

where $Y$ denotes output and $X_i$, $i = 1 \ldots 4$ are the services of equipment, plant, and blue-collar and white-collar workers at time $t$. The function is homogeneous of degree unity in factor inputs. Dual to this production function is a cost function

$$C = C(P_1, P_2, P_3, P_4, t). \qquad (5.2)$$

A translog approximation homogeneous in form to the function (5.2) is

$$\ln C = \alpha_0 + \sum_{i=1}^{4} \alpha_i \ln P_i + \tfrac{1}{2} \sum_{i=1}^{4} \sum_{j=1}^{4} \beta_{ij} \ln P_i \ln P_j$$

$$+ \alpha_t t + \sum_{i=1}^{4} \beta_{it} \ln P_i t + \tfrac{1}{2} \beta_{tt} t^2 \qquad (5.3)$$

where inputs are normalized at unity and time at zero in a given year, and $\alpha_i$ and $\beta_{ij}$ are parameters.[2] Inputs are measured negatively by convention, implying the restrictions

$$\sum_{i=1}^{4} \alpha_i = -1 \text{ and } \sum_{j=1}^{4} \beta_{ij} = 0 \text{ for homogeneity.}$$

The input demands are

$$v_i = \alpha_i + \sum_{j=1}^{4} \beta_{ij} \ln P_j + \beta_{it} t \qquad i = 1 \ldots 4 \qquad (5.4)$$

where $v_i$ is the share of the $i$th input in total production costs. The equilibrium condition in technology yields

$$v_t = \alpha_t + \sum_{j=1}^{4} \beta_{tj} \ln P_j + \beta_{tt} t \qquad (5.5)$$

where

$$v_t = \partial \ln Y / \partial t - \sum_{i=1}^{4} v_i \, \partial \ln X_i / \partial t$$

the rate of growth of total factor productivity or the difference between the growth rates of outputs and inputs weighted by relative shares. The system of equations (5.4) and (5.5) characterizes producer equilibrium, with logarithmic marginal products of factors being equated to cost shares.

The translog approximation is locally monotone if output is increasing with increases in inputs or decreasing with decreases in inputs. Given that inputs are measured as negative outputs, this implies

$$-\alpha_i \geq 0 \qquad i = 1 \ldots 4 \qquad (5.6)$$

at the point [1] for inputs. Locally convex production requires that the associated Hessian matrix be positive definite. For the translog form, this requires convexity of the matrix with typical element

$$\beta_{ii} + \alpha_i(\alpha_i - 1) \qquad i = j$$

$$\beta_{ij} + \alpha_i\alpha_j \qquad i \neq j, i, j = 1 \ldots 4 \qquad (5.7)$$

at the point [1] for inputs.[3]

Conditional on the satisfaction of the regularity conditions, various hypotheses on the form of technical change can be considered. A production function belongs to the class exhibiting factor augmentation if technical change acts in a multiplicative form to shift the efficiency level of each factor. Factor augmentation provides the starting point for the consideration of relative changes in input efficiency levels.

Factor-augmenting technical change implies that the production function (5.1) can be expressed

$$Y = G(A_1X_1, A_2X_2, A_3X_3, A_4X_4) \qquad (5.8)$$

where $A_i$, $i = 1 \ldots 4$ is the augmentation factor associated with the $i$th input.[4] The dual cost function to this is

$$C = C(X_1/A_1, X_2/A_2, X_3/A_3, X_4/A_4).$$

By specifying exponential forms for these rates

$$A_i = e^{\lambda_i t} \qquad (5.9)$$

constant growth rates of disembodied technical change can be associated with each factor. A homogeneous translog to the cost function, given (5.9) is

$$\ln C = \alpha_0 + \sum_{i=1}^{4} \alpha_i \ln P_i + \sum_{i=1}^{4} \alpha_i \lambda_i t$$

$$+ \frac{1}{2} \sum_{i=1}^{4} \sum_{j=1}^{4} \beta_{ij} \ln P_i \ln P_j$$

$$+ \sum_{i=1}^{4} \sum_{j=1}^{4} \beta_{ij} \lambda_j \ln P_i t$$

$$+ \frac{1}{2} \sum_{i=1}^{4} \sum_{j=1}^{4} \beta_{ij} \lambda_i \lambda_j t^2 \tag{5.10}$$

implying the parametric restrictions

$$\alpha_t = \sum_{i=1}^{4} \alpha_i \lambda_i \tag{5.11}$$

$$\beta_{it} = \sum_{j=1}^{4} \beta_{ij} \lambda_j \tag{5.12}$$

$$\beta_{tt} = \sum_{i=1}^{4} \sum_{j=1}^{4} \beta_{ij} \lambda_i \lambda_j \tag{5.13}$$

involving one restriction on the parameters of (5.2) given

$$\sum_{i=1}^{4} \beta_{it} = 0.$$

Given factor augmentation, more restrictive forms of technical change can be imposed on the factor-specific disembodiment parameters. These tests of groupwise equality on a subset of the rates permit the consideration of relative bias in the demand for inputs. For the four-factor case, there are six tests of pairwise equality of augmentation rates. If two mutually exclusive pairings can be imposed, the number of technical change parameters can be reduced to two. If all rates of augmentation are equal, Hicks augmentation characterizes the effect of technical change on the demand for inputs. The structure of technological change so developed is indicated in Figure 5.1, where the notation $E$, $P$, $B$, and $W$ refers to equipment, plant, blue-collar workers, and white-collar workers, respectively.

The capital grouping specifies $\lambda_E = \lambda_P$, or the acceptance of a single capital index of disembodied technical change. A disembodiment index for labor inputs can be constructed if $\lambda_B = \lambda_W$. If both

**Figure 5.1**    Structure of Technological Change

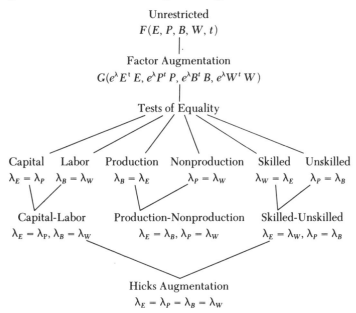

Unrestricted
$$F(E, P, B, W, t)$$

Factor Augmentation
$$G(e^{\lambda E^t} E, e^{\lambda P^t} P, e^{\lambda B^t} B, e^{\lambda W^t} W)$$

Tests of Equality

Capital    Labor    Production    Nonproduction    Skilled    Unskilled
$\lambda_E = \lambda_P$    $\lambda_B = \lambda_W$    $\lambda_B = \lambda_E$    $\lambda_P = \lambda_W$    $\lambda_W = \lambda_E$    $\lambda_P = \lambda_B$

Capital-Labor    Production-Nonproduction    Skilled-Unskilled
$\lambda_E = \lambda_P, \lambda_B = \lambda_W$    $\lambda_E = \lambda_B, \lambda_P = \lambda_W$    $\lambda_E = \lambda_W, \lambda_P = \lambda_B$

Hicks Augmentation
$$\lambda_E = \lambda_P = \lambda_B = \lambda_W$$

pairs of restrictions are accepted, single indices of capital and labor augmentation can be imposed. Such a specification reduces the number of augmentation rates to two, one for labor and one for capital. If these parameters are equal, there is a single rate of disembodied technical change.

As an alternative to the capital services index, it has been hypothesized that technical change causes relative equipment augmentation, or that $\lambda_E > \lambda_P$.[5] A stronger version is absolute white-collar augmentation and blue-collar diminution, or $\lambda_W > 0 > \lambda_B$. The services of structures include those provided by land and buildings, while the services of equipment include machine services and inventory adjustments. If technological change is saving in relatively fixed resources, then differential augmentation of capital goods will obtain. In addition, technological change can be localized in the sense that innovations are most rapid in capital-intensive regions of input space.[6] Given that equipment production is relatively more capital-intensive than structures production, technical change will be relatively equipment using with respect to plant under localized technical progress.

An alternative hypothesis suggesting differential augmentation rates for labor inputs is that of relative augmentation of white-collar with respect to blue-collar labor.[7] A stronger hypothesis is absolute white-collar augmentation and blue-collar diminution, or $\lambda_W > 0 > \lambda_B$. An adaptive advantage is accorded white-collar labor in the implementation of new techniques, given the relative level of skill possessed by this group. In addition, white-collar labor is relatively able to innovate and develop new inventions.[8] A consequence of these relative advantages in adaptation and innovation is that the services of a given man-hour of white-collar labor are augmented at a greater rate than those of a man-hour of blue-collar labor. An additional causal factor is the possibility of localized technical progress in skill-intensive regions of input space, inducing relative white-collar-using techniques.

For this classification, production inputs are assumed to include equipment and blue-collar labor. A production index of technical change can be constructed if the rates of disembodiment for these factors are equal. Nonproduction inputs or overhead factors are plant and white-collar labor. If the equality restrictions implied by indices of production and nonproduction inputs can be accepted simultaneously, the number of augmentation parameters in the specification can be reduced to two. If these separate production and nonproduction augmentation rates are equal, a single augmentation rate can be imposed, yielding the Hicks augmentation case.

For the production grouping, the construction of a technology index is violated if technical change is absolutely equipment augmenting and blue-collar diminishing, since this implies $\lambda_E > 0 > \lambda_B$. Similarly, absolute skill augmentation and plant diminution requires $\lambda_W > 0 > \lambda_P$, preventing the construction of a nonproduction index of technology. It is possible to construct disembodied technical change indices for production and nonproduction inputs if relative equipment augmentation with respect to structures and relative white-collar augmentation with respect to blue-collar workers are accepted, since these restrictions do not constrain the relative rates $(\lambda_B - \lambda_E)$ and $(\lambda_W - \lambda_P)$.

Skilled services used in production are provided by equipment and white-collar workers. There is a single skill-augmenting rate if there is no augmentation differential between these factors. Conversely, unskilled services are provided by blue-collar workers and plant.

### Input Aggregation

The aggregation of a group of inputs requires that all partial elasticities of substitution between a factor within the group and a given factor outside the group be equal for homothetic production.[9] The elasticity of substitution definition on the function (5.2) is

$$\sigma_{ij} = \frac{CC_{ij}}{C_i C_j} \tag{5.14}$$

between factors $i$ and $j$, $i, j = 1 \ldots 4$. For the translog approximation at the point [1] and with time zero,

$$\sigma_{ij} = \frac{\alpha_i \alpha_j + \beta_{ij}}{\alpha_i \alpha_j} \qquad i \neq j \, i, j = 1 \ldots 4 \tag{5.15}$$

with the own $\sigma_{ii}$ solved by the aggregation condition $\Sigma_{j=1}^4 \, \sigma_{ij} \alpha_j = 0$.[10] This reparameterization is expressible in the one-to-one form on the $\beta_{ij}$, $i \neq j$.

$$\beta_{ij} = \rho_{ij} \alpha_j = (\sigma_{ij} - 1) \, \alpha_i \alpha_j \tag{5.16}$$

where $\rho_{ij}$ is the compensated price elasticity of demand for factor $j$ with respect to factor $i$, with the origin translated to the point unity. Separability of $j$ and $k$ from $i$ requires $\sigma_{ij} = \sigma_{ik}$, or in terms of the parameters of the first equality in (5.16),

$$\rho_i = \rho_{ij} = \rho_{ik} \tag{5.17}$$

or that $j$ and $k$ are expressible as a factor aggregate. A stronger version of that hypothesis is explicit separability of $j$ and $k$ from $i$, requiring $\sigma_{ij} = \sigma_{ik} = 1$ or equivalently $\rho_i = 0$. Consequently, by reparameterizing in terms of the elasticities of substitution or elasticities of factor demand, various restrictions of aggregative forms can be tested, through reparameterization of the $\beta_{ij}$ in terms of $\sigma_{ij}$ or $\rho_{ij}$.

There are six pairings for the four-factor classification. The first group to be considered is the separable pairing of equipment and plant $K(E, P)$, implying the existence of a capital aggregate. Such a capital aggregate, separable from the labor services of blue- and white-collar workers can be constructed if $\sigma_{EB} = \sigma_{PB}$ and $\sigma_{EW} = \sigma_{PW}$, where $\sigma_{ij}$ is the partial elasticity of substitution between factors $i$ and $j$.[11] An alternative pairing is an aggregate of labor $L(B, W)$ separable from plant and equipment. An index of labor services can be constructed if $\sigma_{BP} = \sigma_{PW}$ and $\sigma_{BE} = \sigma_{WE}$. If both indices exist simultaneously, then the conventional production inputs of capital and labor can be imposed. The specification of such a function reduces the number of unrestricted cross-partial elasticities of substitution in the model to three, one between labor inputs, one between capital inputs, and one between capital and labor. Subsequently, further equality restrictions on the three elasticities can be imposed to test such forms as the CES and Cobb-Douglas.

The testing of such separate capital and labor aggregates is performed in parallel, with the appropriate restrictions on the elasticities of substitution imposed. This form of production indexing tests for composites of nonhuman and human services. An alternative grouping of inputs is into production and nonproduction classes. A nonproduction aggregate of plant and white-collar services implies that an aggregate of overhead or relatively fixed inputs can be formed, separable from equipment and blue-collar workers. In parallel, for the given specification, a production index of equipment and blue-collar workers can be constructed if these inputs are perfect substitutes or complements in production.[12]

If both production and nonproduction aggregates are accepted, with the implied elasticity restrictions, there are three unrestricted cross-partial elasticities. One elasticity obtains between inputs used in production directly, and another between overhead inputs. A third elasticity measures the substitutability between production and nonproduction indices. As for the case of the capital and labor groupings, more restrictive CES and Cobb-Douglas specifications can be imposed.

An alternative form for aggregating productive inputs is to test for a composite of skilled inputs.[13] Such an index for this specification can be constructed as an aggregate of equipment and white-collar labor. Equipment can be interpreted as a perfect substitute for the productive services of white-collar workers or used in fixed proportion with this labor category in production. Analogously, an unskilled factor composite of blue-collar workers and plant, separable from equipment and white-collar workers, can be tested in parallel. If the two indices are accepted, the list of inputs can be truncated to include skilled and unskilled aggregates. There are three elasticities of substitution, within skilled inputs, within unskilled inputs, and between skilled and unskilled inputs. The CES and Cobb-Douglas specifications can subsequently be tested. The structure of input aggregation in testing for capital and labor, production and nonproduction, and skilled and unskilled aggregates is indicated in Figure 5.2.

Considering the elasticities of substitution, alternative hypotheses of pairwise inequality can be proposed that would prevent the construction of the implied aggregate. One such hypothesis, an alternative to that of the capital composite, is that of relative equipment-labor substitutability.[14] An increase in the relative price of a labor service leads to increased equipment-plant ratios. Causal factors are the relative variability in utilization rates for machinery, and relatively lower adjustment costs in delivery and installation. The hypothesis of equipment labor substitutability consequently proposes $\sigma_{EB} > \sigma_{PB}$, $\sigma_{EW} > \sigma_{PW}$ or rejection of the capital aggregate.

An alternative hypothesis for the elasticities associated with the labor index is capital-skill complementarity.[15] Each capital good is assumed to be complementary with white collar as opposed to blue-collar labor. A relative version of this hypothesis implies $\sigma_{PB} > \sigma_{PW}$ and $\sigma_{EB} > \sigma_{EW}$ or relative complementarity. A stronger or absolute

**Figure 5.2.**    Input Aggregation

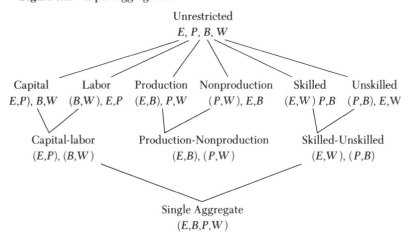

version implies pure complementarity between capital goods and skills, or $\sigma_{PB} > 0 > \sigma_{PW}$, $\sigma_{EB} > 0 > \sigma_{EW}$. A decrease in the relative price of a capital good leads to increased skill intensity in production. The relative and absolute forms of the hypotheses can be tested by imposing the most restrictive aggregate and examining the unrestricted elasticities. The acceptance of the capital aggregate implies the rejection of relative equipment-labor substitutability, and the acceptance of the labor aggregate implies the rejection of relative capital-skill complementarity.

Alternative hypotheses on the partial elasticities can also be constructed for the production aggregate, which requires that $\sigma_{EW} = \sigma_{BW}$ and $\sigma_{EP} = \sigma_{PW}$. In general, it is hypothesized that labor inputs are highly substitutable in production.[16] If capital is relatively complementary with skilled labor, $\sigma_{BW} > \sigma_{EW}$, while if $\sigma_{EW} = \sigma_{BW} \neq 0$, absolute capital-skill complementarity for equipment is rejected without the necessary rejection of labor substitutability. A further alternative is complementarity of white-collar labor with both blue-collar labor and equipment, providing a test of the manpower requirements, or fixed coefficients approach, to calculating skill demands.[17] If $\sigma_{EW} = \sigma_{BW} = 0$, then the hypotheses of capital-skill complementarity, manpower requirements, and production aggregation are all accepted, while labor substitutability is rejected.

It has been hypothesized that plant and equipment are highly complementary in a production structure where labor inputs are included.[18] Causal factors include relative inflexibility of capital goods or putty-clay technologies, and adjustment costs of ordering and installation, which differ between capital goods.[19] Consequently, if $\sigma_{EP} = \sigma_{PW} \leq 0$, then plant is complementary with both equipment and skilled workers. An alternative hypothesis is that of relative substitutability between plant and equipment.[20] This implies $\sigma_{EP} > \sigma_{PW}$ if plant and skill are relatively complementary.

For the nonproduction aggregate of white-collar workers and plant, separable from equipment and blue-collar workers, $\sigma_{EW} = \sigma_{EP}$ and $\sigma_{EW} = \sigma_{PB}$. Complementarity of capital goods and of equipment and skill is testable by $\sigma_{EW} = \sigma_{EP} \leq 0$, and substitutability of labor components and of plant and blue-collar workers is testable by $\sigma_{EW} = \sigma_{PB} > 0$.

The skill aggregate requires $\sigma_{EB} = \sigma_{EW}$ and $\sigma_{EP} = \sigma_{PW}$ as restrictions on the partial elasticities of substitution. If labor groups are relatively complementary and equipment substitutable for blue-collar workers, $\sigma_{BW} > \sigma_{EB}$, and if capital goods are relatively substitutable and capital complementary with skill, $\sigma_{EP} > \sigma_{PW}$. These hypotheses can be tested by consideration of the substitution elasticities. For the unskilled aggregate of blue-collar labor and plant $\sigma_{BW} = \sigma_{PW}$ and $\sigma_{EB} = \sigma_{EP}$. If labor skills are highly substitutable and plant complementary with white-collar labor, then $\sigma_{BW} > \sigma_{PW}$, while if capital goods are relatively complementary and equipment relatively substitutable for blue-collar labor, $\sigma_{EB} > \sigma_{EP}$.

The various hypotheses on the elasticities of substitution are testable by imposing the most restrictive form of input aggregate and subsequently examining the free elasticities in the model.

### Stochastic Specification

The estimation of the system is performed by adding disturbances to the four equations (5.4) and the temporal relation (5.5). Given that observed shares sum to negative unity, there is a linear dependence in the disturbances, implying that one demand equation can be eliminated from the system. The tests for monotonicity and convexity are applied to this four-equation system. The first test for technical change aggregation is that of factor augmentation, derived by the reparameterization of (5.11) through (5.13). Conditional on the acceptance of factor augmentation, the remaining equality restrictions in Figure 5.1 can be imposed and tested.

In parallel, the tests for input aggregation are applied by imposing the reparameterization (5.16) one-to-one in the $\beta_{ij}$, in either $\sigma_{ij}$ or $\rho_{ij}$. Subsequently the test structure of Figure 5.2 can be implemented as restrictions on the elasticities of substitution.

Test statistics for equality restrictions are constructed by computing twice the reduction in the maximized value of the logarithmic likelihood function with restrictions imposed. These likelihood ratios are asymptotically distributed as $\chi^2$ with degrees of freedom equal to the number of restrictions tested. For tests of inequalities, as in the case of monotonicity and convexity, the ratio of the appropriate parameter estimate to its standard error is used to construct a test statistic asymptotically distributed as the standard normal variate.

An overall level of significance of .06 is assigned to the testing of all hypotheses in the model, of which .01 is allocated to the testing of monotonicity and convexity. The remaining .05 serves as an upper bound for the testing of indices of technical change and factor inputs. Critical values for the $\chi^2$/degrees of freedom and standard normal variates are illustrated in Table 5.1 If interpolation of the significance level is required, this is performed linearly on the logarithms of the upper and lower significance bounds.

### Empirical Results

The test structure is applied to data on equipment, plant, blue-collar and white-collar inputs for the U.S. private domestic economy, 1948–1972. Plant includes land and nonresidential structures services. The data for equipment and plant are from Christensen and Jorgenson (1973). Blue-collar and white-collar labor input series are constructed from the data described in previous chapters.[21] The indices are normalized at unity in 1958, with time normalized at zero in that year and quantity levels of inputs assumed exogenous.

The tests for the conditions of monotonicity and convexity are indicated in Table 5.2. There are four inequalities tested for each condition, with a significance level of .001 assigned to each statistic constructed. The test statistics are formed as the ratio of a given

**Table 5.1.** Critical Values of $\chi^2$/Degrees of Freedom (D.F.) and Standard Normal (S.N.) Variate

| Degrees of Freedom | Critical Value of $\chi^2$/D.F. | | | | |
| | Significance Level | | | | |
| | .05 | .025 | .01 | .005 | .001 |
| --- | --- | --- | --- | --- | --- |
| 1 | 3.84 | 5.02 | 6.63 | 7.88 | 10.83 |
| 2 | 3.00 | 3.69 | 4.61 | 5.30 | 6.91 |
| 3 | 2.60 | 3.12 | 3.78 | 4.28 | 5.43 |
| 4 | 2.37 | 2.79 | 3.32 | 3.72 | 4.63 |
| 5 | 2.21 | 2.57 | 3.02 | 3.35 | 4.12 |
| 6 | 2.10 | 2.41 | 2.80 | 3.09 | 3.75 |
| S.N. | | | | | |
| ∞ | 1.65 | 1.96 | 2.33 | 2.58 | 3.09 |

**Table 5.2.**    Monotonicity and Convexity Tests, Production Aggregation

| Parametric Restriction | Test Statistic (S.N.) |
|---|---|
| Monotonicity | |
| $-\alpha_W \geq 0$ | 93.74 |
| $-\alpha_B \geq 0$ | 110.69 |
| $-\alpha_E \geq 0$ | 25.24 |
| $-\alpha_P \geq 0$ | 20.43 |
| Convexity | |
| $\delta_{WW} \geq 0$ | 13.04 |
| $\delta_{BB} \geq 0$ | 10.57 |
| $\delta_{EE} \geq 0$ | 4.47 |
| $\delta_{PP} \geq 0$ | 3.02 |

parameter estimate to its standard error, distributed asymptotically as the standard normal estimate. If any of the four conditions of the form (5.6) is less than $-3.09$, the production function is rejected as being locally monotone. At the given significance level, output is shown to be increasing in the levels of all inputs. Applying the same level of significance to the testing of locally convex production, this regulatory condition is accepted. The $\delta_{ii}$ elements in Table 5.2 denote the elements of the diagonalized matrix constructed from the Hessian matrix (5.7). Production can consequently be characterized by a well-behaved translog approximation to an underlying function.

Given monotonicity and convexity, the test structure for the form of technological change is applied. The test statistics are reported in Table 5.3 for factor augmentation and subsequent equality restrictions on the augmentation parameters. Factor augmentation involves the reparameterization of (5.11) through (5.13), involving one restriction on the temporal parameters. At a level of .01 with one degree of freedom, factor augmentation is accepted. Technical change can be represented by factor-specific shifts in efficiency levels, given an exponential form of the nature of augmentation. Given that the maximal significance level for tests on the form of technical change and aggregation is .05, an upper bound of .04 can be allocated to testing the equality hypotheses, conditional on factor augmentation.

**Table 5.3.**   Test Statistics, Technological Change

| Test | Parametric Restrictions | D.F. | $\chi^2/$D.F. |
|------|------------------------|------|---------------|
| Factor Augmentation | | 1 | 3.09 |
| Test of Equality | | | |
| *Single Pairings* | | | |
| Capital | $\lambda_E = \lambda_P$ | 1 | 1.93 |
| Labor | $\lambda_B = \lambda_W$ | 1 | 1.44 |
| Production | $\lambda_B = \lambda_E$ | 1 | 2.13 |
| Nonproduction | $\lambda_P = \lambda_W$ | 1 | 2.13 |
| Skilled | $\lambda_W = \lambda_E$ | 1 | 2.22 |
| Unskilled | $\lambda_B = \lambda_P$ | 1 | 0.03 |
| *Two Pairings* | | | |
| Capital-Labor | $\lambda_E = \lambda_P, \lambda_B = \lambda_W$ | 2 | 0.97 |
| Production Nonproduction | $\lambda_B = \lambda_E, \lambda_W = \lambda_P$ | 2 | 0.67 |
| Skilled-Unskilled | $\lambda_W = \lambda_E, \lambda_B = \lambda_P$ | 2 | 1.58 |
| Single Index | | | |
| Hicks Augmentation | $\lambda_E = \lambda_P = \lambda_B = \lambda_W$ | 3 | 2.26 |

All pairwise technical change indices, imposed separately, are accepted at the .01 level. The implication is that all forms imposing mutually exclusive pairings of augmentation factors are accepted, as indicated in Table 5.3. Hicks augmentation is implied by the simultaneous acceptance of all six pairwise forms, and this is accepted at a level of .01.

An implication of this form of augmentation is that given homogeneity of the translog approximation the sole effect of disembodied technical change is to act as an efficiency shift of the quantity of output. By measuring output in efficiency units and normalizing by this index, the resulting demand model can be expressed independently of time.[22] Alternatively, factor inputs are strongly separable from time, and output can be expressed as the sum of two functions, one aggregating factor inputs, and the other representing time.

In addition, all forms of relative and absolute augmentation rate differentials are rejected. In particular, technical change is not relatively augmenting in white-collar workers.[23] Moreover, technical change is not relatively equipment augmenting with respect to the services of plant.[24]

The tests for aggregative forms, using the structure of Figure 5.2, are detailed in Table 5.4. The first procedure is to test for the six separate input pairings, which are considered in parallel. The parametric restrictions are indicated, with the number of degrees of freedom being equal to the number of restrictions. The tests for an aggregative structure are performed in parallel with those for the form of technical change, implying that an upper bound of .05 is the significance level allocated for hypothesis testing. At a level of .05, the production and nonproduction pairings are accepted separately, and the remaining four pairwise specifications are rejected. The test for

**Table 5.4.** Test Statistics, Production Aggregation

| Test | Parametric Restrictions | $\chi^2$/D.F. |
|------|-------------------------|---------------|
| Input Pairings | | |
| Capital | $\sigma_{PW} = \sigma_{EW}, \sigma_{PB} = \sigma_{EB}$ | 9.37 |
| Labor | $\sigma_{PW} = \sigma_{PB}, \sigma_{EW} = \sigma_{EB}$ | 10.74 |
| Production | $\sigma_{EW} = \sigma_{BW}, \sigma_{PE} = \sigma_{PB}$ | 1.37 |
| Nonproduction | $\sigma_{EW} = \sigma_{PE}, \sigma_{BW} = \sigma_{PB}$ | 0.16 |
| Skilled | $\sigma_{PE} = \sigma_{PW}, \sigma_{EB} = \sigma_{BW}$ | 3.42 |
| Unskilled | $\sigma_{PE} = \sigma_{EB}, \sigma_{PW} = \sigma_{BW}$ | 4.64 |
| Two Pairings | | |
| Capital-Labor | $\sigma_{PW} = \sigma_{PB} = \sigma_{EW} = \sigma_{EB}$ | 8.02 |
| Production-Nonproduction | $\sigma_{EW} = \sigma_{BW} = \sigma_{PE} = \sigma_{PB}$ | 0.97 |
| Skilled-Unskilled | $\sigma_{PE} = \sigma_{PW} = \sigma_{BW} = \sigma_{EB}$ | 4.76 |
| Single Aggregate | | |
| CES | $\sigma = \sigma_{BW} = \sigma_{PB} = \sigma_{EW}$ $= \sigma_{PE} = \sigma_{EB} = \sigma_{PW}$ | 9.11 |
| Cobb-Douglas | $\sigma = 1$ | 10.77 |

the production-nonproduction aggregate is consequently performed, given that the separate component subaggregates are accepted. At a level of .01, this aggregate is accepted, as indicated in the second group of results in Table 5.4. The rejection of the capital and labor groupings, and of the two-skill aggregates, implies the rejection of the two-pairings specification associated with each. For completeness, the test statistics for these aggregates are indicated. The acceptance of a single production aggregate requires the acceptance of all pairwise specifications. At a level of .01, both the CES and Cobb-Douglas specifications are rejected. Consequently, the production-nonproduction specification is imposed.

The implication is that inputs can be grouped into composites representing overhead and process factors. For this specification, overhead or nonproduction factors are white-collar labor and plant, also the factors relatively fixed in production. Equipment and blue-collar labor, relatively variable factors in production, can be similarly expressed as a process or production aggregate.

It remains to present the parameter estimates for the elasticities of substitution, indicated in Table 5.5 for the unrestricted case and with the production-nonproduction aggregate imposed. From the results for this latter case, plant is relatively more complementary with white-collar than with blue-collar labor, while equipment is relatively more complementary with blue-collar labor. As a consequence, no conclusive evidence of capital–white-collar complementarity is obtained. At constant relative wages by skill there is not necessarily an increase in the relative quantity of skilled labor.[25] White-collar labor is equally substitutable with equipment and plant, but blue-collar labor is more substitutable with plant than with equipment. Absolute plant–white-collar complementarity is evidenced by the negative elasticity estimate.

An alternative estimate of the elasticity of substitution, between plant and equipment of 1.72 has been presented by Boddy and Gort (1971). The data base is the U.S. private business economy, 1902–1968, indicating a definition similar to that used here.[26] Sato (1967), using a two-level CES, obtains an estimate of 1.63 for U.S. manufacturing for 1929–1963. Both estimates are similar to the 1.84 derived for the production-nonproduction aggregate, indicating substitutability between plant and equipment. Considering labor, similar estimates indicating high substitutability between categories have been

**Table 5.5.**   Elasticity of Substitution Parameter Estimates

| Elasticity of Substitution | Unrestricted | Production-Nonproduction Aggregate Imposed |
|---|---|---|
| $\sigma_{PE}$ | 1.98 | 1.84 |
| | (3.30) | (.05) |
| $\sigma_{PB}$ | 2.27 | 2.17 |
| | (.83) | (.77) |
| $\sigma_{PW}$ | −2.42 | −3.26 |
| | (1.21) | (.79) |
| $\sigma_{BW}$ | 1.88 | 1.84 |
| | (.17) | (.05) |
| $\sigma_{EW}$ | .73 | 1.84 |
| | (.64) | (.05) |
| $\sigma_{EB}$ | −.18 | .62 |
| | (.59) | (.37) |

obtained.[27] These estimates are generally higher than that reported here, as a consequence of the selected aggregation.

The implications of various economic policy changes can be considered in the context of the results of the elasticity of substitution estimates. An investment tax credit to subsidize the purchase of equipment reduces the user cost of such services.[28] Given that the elasticity of substitution between equipment and white-collar workers exceeds that between equipment and blue-collar workers, the increase in equipment demand will be associated with a relative decrease in the demand for white-collar relative to blue-collar labor.

An alternative policy change is the introduction of a tax credit for property taxes paid, as opposed to a deduction in the calculation of taxable income. Such a policy reduces the user cost of plant, causing these goods to be substituted for equipment. Given that plant and white-collar workers are pure complements, the absolute employment level for this category increases, while plant is substituted for blue-collar workers.

In conclusion, the empirical results support the aggregation into two separable composites of inputs used in processing and overhead inputs. For these composites, white-collar workers and plant are complementary within the nonproduction index, and unskilled workers and equipment are complementary within the production index, given the elasticity estimates. Although within-group complementarity obtains, the elasticity of substitution between production and nonproduction inputs is significantly greater than unity. For the elasticities, white-collar labor is relatively more substitutable with equipment than with plant, while blue-collar labor is relatively more substitutable with plant than with equipment. This suggests that, although the skill aggregates are rejected, equipment is indicated to be relatively more white-collar intensive than plant.

Two hypotheses proposed to explain observed increases in equipment intensity have been examined, namely those of relative equipment labor substitutability and relative equipment augmentation. The first is supported for white-collar but not for blue-collar workers, given the rejection of the labor aggregate, while the second is rejected. For labor, analogous hypotheses of capital–white-collar complementarity and relative white-collar augmentation are proposed. The first is supported for plant and rejected for equipment, given the rejection of the capital aggregate, and the second is rejected.

# 6

# HUMAN CAPITAL AND VINTAGE EFFECTS

If a group of factors is perfectly substitutable or complementary in production, the group can be represented by a single index. A production index of capital services is viewed as an aggregate of plant and equipment of different ages, defined by their dates of manufacture. Analogously, the labor aggregate in production can be interpreted as a composite of the services of workers of different ages. This aggregate can be viewed as a human capital index, with constituent components being the services of workers classified by age.[1]

In this context, production rejects a labor aggregate if there is an increase in the relative demand for a given age group at constant relative wages, or if fixed proportions of age groups are not used in production. A test can be performed as to whether there is a single index of technical change for human capital services. For homothetic production, the possibility of substitution between inputs at a given level of technology can be tested as to whether the partial elasticities of substitution between physical capital and each age group are unequal. Alternatively, such inequalities among elasticities prevent the construction of an aggregate labor index in production.

Empirical evidence on the demand for labor by age suggests substitutability of capital for newer or younger workers.[2] One issue is to determine whether this substitutability for capital is relatively greater for younger than older workers. In addition, if it is observed that relative wages by age are constant while relative quantities of labor services are not constant, a possible explanation can be derived through unequal partial elasticities of substitution by age, or unequal relative rates of augmentation.

Human capital can be interpreted as an aggregate of education or formal schooling and experience, or, alternatively, of general and specific skills.[3] Since different age groups embody varying proportions of the two components, the substitutability of these skills in production can be considered by examining substitution by age. In particular, education decreases monotonically and experience increases monotonically with age. Consequently, the substitution between young and old workers surrogates the substitution of general and specific skills. Moreover, given that human capital increases with age and subsequently decreases, by denoting the region of the stock peak as middle age, substitution of these three age groups can be considered.[4]

The procedure for testing commences with a production function with factor inputs representing physical capital services and the services of three labor groups, younger, middle-aged, and older workers. Restrictions on the function implied by various indices of technology are imposed. Specifically, the restrictions implied by factor augmentation and equal pairwise rates of disembodied technical progress are examined. The most restrictive index accepted is imposed.

For substitution possibilities, a test is performed for the existence of the human capital aggregate. Partial forms of aggregation involving two human capital services can be tested. The procedure is to impose the parametric restrictions on the elasticities of substitution for various aggregate forms, and to impose the most restrictive of these.

The tests are applied to data for the U.S. private domestic economy for 1948–1972. From the elasticity of substitution estimates, such hypotheses as capital substitutability for young workers and complementarity with human capital-intensive workers can be examined. In addition, the substitution between education and experience in production, and the impact of such policies affecting labor demand by age as minimum wage and social security legislation can be considered.

## Technological Change

The starting point in the examination of hypotheses concerning the role of technical change is the consideration of a production function with physical and human capital services as inputs. Let production be represented by the function

$$Y = F(X_1, X_2, X_3, X_4, t) \tag{6.1}$$

where $Y$ denotes output and $X_i$, $i = 1 \ldots 4$ are, respectively, the services of physical capital and the human capital services provided by younger, middle-aged, and older workers at time $t$. Dual to this production funetion is a cost function

$$C = C(P_1, P_2, P_3, P_4, t) \tag{6.2}$$

where the $P$ elements denote prices of the services consumed in production. A translog approximation to the function (6.2) is

$$\ln C = \alpha_0 + \sum_{i=1}^{4} \alpha_i \ln P_i + \tfrac{1}{2} \sum_{i=1}^{4} \sum_{j=1}^{4} \beta_{ij} \ln P_i \ln P_j$$
$$+ \alpha_t t + \sum_{i=1}^{4} \beta_{it} \ln P_i t + \tfrac{1}{2} \beta_{tt} t^2 \tag{6.3}$$

where inputs are normalized at unity and time at zero in a given year and the Greek notation designates parameters.[5] The approximation is assumed to be homogeneous around the point of expansion.[6] The demands for physical and human capital can be expressed as

$$S_i = \alpha_i + \sum_{j=1}^{4} \beta_{ij} \ln P_j + \beta_{it} t \qquad i = 1 \ldots 4 \tag{6.4}$$

where $S_i$, the relative share in total cost of the $i$th factor, is equated with the logarithmic marginal product of that factor. Differentiating (6.3) in time yields

$$S_t = \alpha_t \sum_{j=1}^{4} \beta_{tj} \ln P_j + \beta_{tt} t \tag{6.5}$$

where, as an alternative formulation

$$S_t = \partial \ln Y / \partial t - \sum_{i=1}^{4} S_i \partial \ln X_i / \partial t$$

is the rate of growth of total factor productivity, the difference between the growth of output and the share-weighted growth of inputs. Moreover, if the specification for the shares in compensation follows the two-period arithmetic mean moving average, then this is exact for the translog form. From the demand equations (6.4) and (6.5), various parametric restrictions can be imposed.

Factor augmentation implies that the production function can be expressed as

$$Y = G(A_1 X_1, A_2 X_2, A_3 X_3, A_4 X_4)$$

with the dual cost function being

$$C = C(X_1/A_1, X_2/A_2, X_3/A_3, X_4/A_4) \tag{6.6}$$

where $A_i$, $i = 1 \ldots 4$ is a shift term associated with disembodied technical change for the $i$th factor.[7] The factor augmentation form provides a convenient form to test further parametric restrictions on technical change. A parametric specification is an exponential form, or

$$A_i = e^{\lambda_i t} \qquad i = 1 \ldots 4 \tag{6.7}$$

with $\lambda_i$ representing the constant rate of disembodied technical change for the $i$th factor.

A homogeneous translog approximation to (6.6) is

$$\begin{aligned}
\ln C = \alpha_0 &+ \sum_{i-1}^{4} \alpha_i \ln P_i + \sum_{i-1}^{4} \alpha_i \lambda_i t \\
&+ \tfrac{1}{2} \sum_{i-1}^{4} \sum_{j-1}^{4} \beta_{ij} \ln P_i \ln P_j \\
&+ \sum_{i-1}^{4} \sum_{j-1}^{4} \beta_{ij} \lambda_i \lambda_j \ln P_i t \\
&+ \tfrac{1}{2} \sum_{i-1}^{4} \sum_{j-1}^{4} \beta_{ij} \lambda_i \lambda_j t^2
\end{aligned} \tag{6.8}$$

implying the parametric restrictions

$$\alpha_t = \sum_{i-1}^{4} \alpha_i \lambda_i$$

$$\beta_{it} = \sum_{j-1}^{4} \beta_{ij} \lambda_j, \quad \beta_{tt} = \sum_{i-1}^{4} \sum_{j-1}^{4} \beta_{ij} \lambda_i \lambda_j \tag{6.9}$$

involving one restriction on the parameters of (6.3), given

$$\sum_{i=1}^{4} \beta_{it} = 0.$$

An empirical observation for the period up to 1970 for the rental price of human capital services is that the price failed to decrease with increases in the stock of human capital.[8] Relative wages by age remained constant despite a changing composition of employment. Relative increases in employment of younger and middle-aged workers were associated with constancy of relative wages by age.[9] A possible causal factor was the presence of unequal rates of disembodied technical change for human capital services.[10] Specifically, middle-aged or relatively skill-intensive services were augmented at rates higher than those of less skilled cohorts, particularly older workers.

If the technology exhibits relatively using technical change in labor of human capital–intensive ages and against less human capital–intensive ages, the isoquant will exhibit a relatively greater shift toward the origin in skill-intensive regions of input space. Several causal factors can be advanced to support such phenomena. Middle-aged workers, being relatively skilled, possess relatively shorter implementation lags and lower costs of adjustment and information in the adaptation of new inventions. In addition, middle-aged labor, being relatively intensive in the human capital components of education and experience, possesses a relatively greater ability in innovation and the introduction of new techniques.[11] Finally, this observation will occur if technical progress is localized, with innovations relatively abundant in human capital–intensive regions.[12]

For education separately, human capital measured by years of schooling decreases monotonically with age. Skill using technical progress for education implies relative augmentation of the services of younger workers. Human capital measured by experience increases monotonically with age. Relative augmentation for older workers is implied by a relative using bias in experience. The services of experienced workers are augmented at a more rapid rate than is the case with less experienced workers.

The hypothesis to be tested is that relatively skilled middle-aged labor services are augmented at a rate greater than those of older and younger workers. Both relative and absolute effects can be distinguished. Designate the services of physical capital by $k$, and those provided by younger, middle-aged, and older workers by $Y$, $M$, and $S$ respectively. These technical change functions are viewed as shifting the production function outwards if positive, or shifting the cost function downwards toward the origin if positive. Technical change is relatively skill augmenting if $\lambda_M > \lambda_S > \lambda_Y$, that is, if skill definitions are based on absolute wages.[13] This implies that the augmentation rate associated with human capital intensive age groups exceeds that for less skilled groups, without necessarily requiring net augmentation or positive rates for any factor. Absolute effects in favor of skilled and against unskilled age groups occur if $\lambda_M > 0 > \lambda_S > \lambda_Y$, or augmentation occurs for skilled labor and diminution for unskilled labor.

Conditional on factor augmentation, a test for equal augmentation rates can be performed by the restriction $\lambda_Y = \lambda_M = \lambda_S$. Acceptance of such a hypothesis implies that there is a single rate of augmentation for human capital services. This rate can be tested as equal to the rate of augmentation for physical capital services. If this hypothesis of equality of augmentation parameters is accepted, there is a single index of technology augmenting all factors at the same rate. An alternative test is for physical capital augmentation only, with a zero restriction on the human capital rate.

A further series of tests can be performed as to whether technical change augments a single human capital service by imposing zero restrictions on two of the labor technical change parameters.[14]

The most restrictive technical change form acceptable is imposed. The test structure for these hypotheses is indicated in Figure 6.1.

### Substitution Possibilities

Technical change can be assumed to be embodied in labor inputs of different vintages. In this context, the acceptance of a human capital services aggregate implies that all age groups are equally substitutable with physical capital, also implying the absence of embodied vintage effects. A convenient method of testing for embodied vintage effects, then, is to examine the elasticities of substitution between different factors in production.

The elasticity of substitution between factors $i$ and $j$ is

$$\sigma_{ij} = \frac{CC_{ij}}{C_i C_j} \qquad i \neq j, i,j = 1 \ldots 4 \qquad (6.10)$$

where $\sigma_{ij}$ is the elasticity of substitution. For the translog approximation (6.3)

$$\sigma_{ij} = 1 + \frac{\beta_{ij}}{\alpha_i \alpha_j} \qquad (6.11)$$

and the own $\sigma_{ii}$ can be solved by the relation $\Sigma_{j-1}^4 \ \sigma_{ij}\alpha_j = 0$. Consequently, by reparameterizing the $\beta_{ij}$ in terms of $\sigma_{ij}$, the partial elasticities of substitution can be estimated directly.[15] The first procedure is to test for aggregates grouping inputs in a mutually exclusive and exhaustive classification.[16] Aggregates can be constructed if the marginal rate of technical substitution between two inputs in a group is independent of any input outside the group.

Consider all groupings of the four inputs into alternative specifications containing an aggregate of one-factor pairing. There are six forms for such input pairings. Three of these specifications involve a physical and human capital pairing, while the remaining three specifications involve a pairing of two human capital components. An

**Figure 6.1.**   Technical Change in Age Aggregation

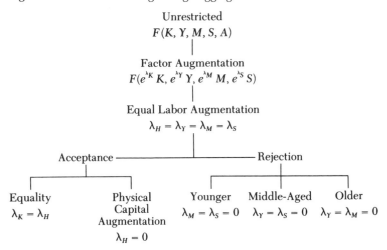

equivalent restriction for aggregation within a homothetic function is equality of all partial elasticities involving one factor within the group and one factor outside the group. The acceptance of any aggregate implies that the original components of the aggregate can be represented by linear combinations of the truncated factor listing.[17]

There are four mutually exclusive and exhaustive specifications involving three factor inputs, one of which is the labor aggregate of human capital. Partial aggregates are implied by the elasticity restrictions in any index of one capital and two labor services. If the human capital aggregate is accepted, the conventional capital and labor indices in production can be utilized. Other specifications are mutually exclusive pairs of aggregates and CES and Cobb-Douglas functions. The forms with associated parametric restrictions are indicated in Table 6.1.

Conditional on the most restrictive vintage index, tests of substitution between ages can be performed, in addition to alternative hypotheses on the relationship between pairwise elasticities of substitution. Consider the factor pairings containing physical capital and one human capital component. A hypothesis supporting the existence of elasticity differentials is that of capital-skill complementarity.[18] In this context, skilled labor is complementary with the age group most intensive in human capital. The hypothesis can assume relative and absolute forms. Relative capital-skill complementarity requires that $\sigma_{KY} > \sigma_{KS} > \sigma_{KM}$. As human capital intensity for a given age group increases, the partial elasticity with physical capital decreases. An absolute version specifies pure complementarity between capital and skilled labor and pure substitutability between capital and unskilled labor, or $\sigma_{KY} > 0$, $\sigma_{KM} \geq 0$, as an additional condition.

Human capital increases with age until middle age and then decreases. There are two forms of testable hypotheses applicable in this case. The first is that substitution elasticities are relatively high for adjacent age cohorts and decrease as age differentials widen.[19] Given that educational attainment decreases monotonically, this implies relative complementarity of education and experience. The second alternative is that substitution elasticities are dependent on human capital intensity, with $\sigma_{YS} > \sigma_{YM}$ and $\sigma_{YS} > \sigma_{MS}$, implying a decrease as human capital differentials increase. For either age or human capital intensity forms, a further proposition is that all partial elasticities of substitution exceed zero significantly.[20]

**Table 6.1.**    Parametric Restrictions, Human Capital Aggregation

| Form | Parametric Restrictions |
|------|------------------------|
| **Three Groups** | |
| $(K, Y), M, S$ | $\sigma_{KM} = \sigma_{YM}, = \sigma_{KS} = \sigma_{YS}$ |
| $(K, M), Y, S$ | $\sigma_{KY} = \sigma_{YM}, = \sigma_{KS} = \sigma_{MS}$ |
| $(K, S), Y, M$ | $\sigma_{KY} = \sigma_{YS}, = \sigma_{KM} = \sigma_{MS}$ |
| $(Y, M), K, S$ | $\sigma_{KY} = \sigma_{KM}, = \sigma_{YS} = \sigma_{MS}$ |
| $(Y, S), K, M$ | $\sigma_{KY} = \sigma_{KS}, = \sigma_{YM} = \sigma_{MS}$ |
| $(M, S), K, Y$ | $\sigma_{KM} = \sigma_{KS}, = \sigma_{YM} = \sigma_{YS}$ |
| **Two Groups** | |
| $(K, Y, M), S$ | $\sigma_{KS} = \sigma_{YS}, = \sigma_{MS}$ |
| $(K, Y, S), M$ | $\sigma_{KM} = \sigma_{YM}, = \sigma_{MS}$ |
| $(K, M, S), Y$ | $\sigma_{KY} = \sigma_{YM}, = \sigma_{YS}$ |
| $(Y, M, S), K$ | $\sigma_{KY} = \sigma_{KM}, = \sigma_{KS}$ |
| $(K, Y), (M, S)$ | $\sigma_{KM} = \sigma_{YM}, = \sigma_{KS} = \sigma_{YS}$ |
| $(K, M), (Y, S)$ | $\sigma_{KY} = \sigma_{YM}, = \sigma_{KS} = \sigma_{MS}$ |
| $(K, S), (Y, M)$ | $\sigma_{KY} = \sigma_{YS}, = \sigma_{KM} = \sigma_{MS}$ |
| **One Group** | |
| CES | $\sigma = \sigma_{ij}, i \neq j, i,j = K, Y, M, S$ |
| Cobb-Douglas | $\sigma = 1$ |

From the index restrictions, substitution possibilities by age and human capital intensity, in addition to such possibilities between specific and general skills, can be considered.

### Empirical Results

The system estimated contains $(n-1)$ equations of the form (6.4), given a linear dependence in the observed shares and associated errors, and the relation (6.5). Tests for disembodied and embodied vintage effects are based respectively on the reparameterizations (6.9) and (6.11). Test statistics for equality restrictions are constructed by computing twice the reduction in the maximized value of the logarithmic likelihood function with restrictions imposed. These likelihood ratio statistics are asymptotically distributed as $\chi^2$ with degrees of freedom equal to the number of restrictions tested.

Critical values of the statistic are illustrated in Table 6.2. An overall level of significance of .05 is assigned to testing hypotheses on substitution possibilities and technical change.

The data used for the tests comprise time series on prices and quantities of labor services by age and capital services for the U.S. private domestic economy for 1948–1972. Younger workers are defined as aged 16–24, middle-aged workers as 25–54, and older workers as 55 and older. The observations on $S_t$ are constructed as the difference between the logarithmic first differences of output and a share-weighted index of inputs. All quantities are indexed at unity in 1958, with time normalized at zero in that year.

**Table 6.2.**   Test Statistics, Technical Change in Age

| Form | | $\mu_K$ | $\mu_M$ | $\mu_S$ | $\lambda_Y$ | D.F. | $\chi^2/$D.F. |
|---|---|---|---|---|---|---|---|
| 1. | Factor Augmentation | −.0218 (.0034) | .0166 (.0012) | .0174 (.0032) | −.0309 (.0247) | 1 | 3.38 |
| 2. | Labor Equality | .0638 (.0699) | | | −.0557 (.0371) | 2 | 6.96 |
| 3. | Equality | | | | .0061 (.0036) | 3 | 6.14 |
| | Physical Capital Augmentation | .0232 (.0218) | | | | 3 | 5.77 |
| 4. | Human Capital Augmentation | | | | | | |
| | Younger | | | | −.0106 (.0025) | 3 | 5.18 |
| | Middle-aged | | .0111 (.0017) | | | 3 | 2.36 |
| | Older | | | −.0169 (.0053) | | 3 | 3.35 |

The first procedure is to test for monotonicity and convexity of the production function locally. At a significance level of .01 both these conditions are satisfied.[21] The remaining .04 serves as an upper bound for testing hypotheses on augmentation and substitution. The results for the testing of technical change as indicated in Figure 6.1 are reported in Table 6.3. The elements $\mu_K$, $\mu_M$, and $\mu_S$ denote, respectively, differentials between the augmentation rates for physical capital, middle-aged, and older workers and the rate for younger workers.

At a level of .025 factor augmentation is accepted, but the additional restriction to the labor equality form is rejected. Consequently, augmentation rates on human capital services are rejected as being equal. These conclusions are derived from the $\chi^2/\text{D.F.}$ statistics

**Table 6.3.**   Test Statistics, Human Capital Aggregation

| Form | Degrees of Freedom (D.F.) | $\chi^2/\text{D.F.}$ |
|---|---|---|
| 1.  Three Groups | | |
| $(K, Y) M, S$ | 2 | 24.55 |
| $(K, M) Y, S$ | 2 | 3.22 |
| $(K, S) Y, M$ | 2 | 17.66 |
| $(Y, M) K, S$ | 2 | 7.28 |
| $(Y, S) K, M$ | 2 | 18.48 |
| $(M, S) K, Y$ | 2 | 13.37 |
| 2.  Two Groups | | |
| $(K, Y, M) S$ | 2 | 10.35 |
| $(K, Y, S) M$ | 2 | 11.69 |
| $(K, M, S) Y$ | 2 | 13.98 |
| $(Y, M, S) K$ | 2 | 7.11 |
| $(K, Y) (M, S)$ | 3 | 17.85 |
| $(K, M) (Y, S)$ | 3 | 14.20 |
| $(K, S) (Y, M)$ | 3 | 7.17 |
| 3.  One Group | | |
| CES | 5 | 9.96 |
| Cobb-Douglas | 6 | 19.27 |

in the last column of Table 6.3. The relative rates of augmentation with respect to younger workers are significantly positive for human capital–intensive age groups.

The model is tested for human capital augmentation in one factor. At a significance level of .025 middle-aged augmentation is accepted and younger and older augmentation rejected. Consequently, this specification is imposed on the model. Technical change augments labor services at different rates, with middle-aged workers, the most human capital–intensive age category, being augmented at a greater rate than other groups. The hypothesis implies that physical capital and the services of less skilled categories are augmented at equal rates. The relative augmentation rate of 1.11 percent per annum is significant at the .01 level.[22] The acceptance of such a hypothesis provides one source of explanation for nondecreasing rates of return to human capital investment.

Of the total significance level, .01 and .025 are respectively assigned to testing the hypotheses on regularity in production and technical change, implying that .015 is the upper bound for testing substitution possibilities. The results of these tests are reported in Table 6.3. The first group of test statistics obtains for all pairwise aggregates containing either physical capital services and the services of one human capital factor, or two human capital components. At a level of .01, the aggregate of capital services and middle-aged labor is accepted, and all remaining pairs are rejected. The second group of tests, for groupings to reduce the number of inputs to two, is tested at a significance level of .01. There are four tests for aggregates of three factors, including the human capital aggregate of younger, middle-aged, and older workers, all of which are rejected. The three specifications involving two pairs of factors are rejected, as are the CES and Cobb-Douglas forms. In conclusion, the tests indicated that a grouping of physical capital and skilled or human capital–intensive labor is accepted, and that the aggregate of heterogeneous human capital inputs is rejected.

Similar results have been obtained for alternative skill aggregates in production. Berndt and Christensen (1974), using a classification by occupation, also reject the hypothesis of labor services aggregation.[23] Bowles (1970) and Welch (1969), classifying labor inputs by education into three categories, are able to truncate the list of inputs, but not into fewer than two labor groups.[24]

The elasticity of substitution estimates are presented in table 6.4. In the first column, parameter estimates for the unrestricted form are indicated, with standard errors in parentheses. Imposing the aggregate of physical capital and the human capital services of middle-aged workers, the restricted estimates are presented in the second column.

**Table 6.4.**  Substitution and Distribution Parameter Estimates

| Parameters | Unrestricted | $(K, M)$ Aggregate Imposed |
|---|---|---|
| $\alpha_K$ | −.3912<br>(.0060) | −.4055<br>(.0032) |
| $\alpha_Y$ | −.0373<br>(.0028) | −.0358<br>(.0027) |
| $\alpha_M$ | −.4623<br>(.0038) | −.4531<br>(.0022) |
| $\alpha_S$ | −.1092<br>(.0015) | −.1056<br>(.0008) |
| $\sigma_{KY}$ | 1.7611<br>(.5471) | 2.7380<br>(.0794) |
| $\sigma_{KM}$ | .5694<br>(.3854) | 1.1193<br>(.1054) |
| $\sigma_{KS}$ | .4275<br>(.3537) | 1.3502<br>(.0975) |
| $\sigma_{YM}$ | 3.1286<br>(.3010) | 2.7380<br>(.0794) |
| $\sigma_{YS}$ | .0219<br>(.5679) | −.9847<br>(.3761) |
| $\sigma_{MS}$ | 1.9463<br>(.2198) | 1.3502<br>(.0975) |

From the results with the most restrictive aggregate imposed, the elasticities of substitution can be examined. The elasticity of substitution between capital and younger workers is 2.74, while that for middle-aged workers is 1.12. Physical capital is consequently relatively complementary with human capital–intensive age groups. A similar conclusion is obtained by comparing the estimates of $\sigma_{KY}$ with $\sigma_{KS}$. This suggests the presence of capital-skill complementarity in production.[25]

Within the human capital services components, decreasing substitutability with age differentials is obtained. The highest elasticity of substitution is between younger and middle-aged workers, followed by that between middle-aged and older workers and finally older and younger workers. The former two pairs are highly substitutable, and the latter pair is complementary. Alternative evidence supporting high elasticity estimates has been presented from occupational and educational classifications.[26] Complementarity between certain types of labor inputs has also been hypothesized.[27] The results suggest that general human capital or education is more substitutable in production than specific human capital, or experience. More specifically, production can be assumed to occur with fixed proportions of workers intensive in experience and education, respectively.

Factors of production relatively more intensive in general human capital are more highly substitutable for each other. Conversely, factors intensive in general human capital are relatively less substitutable for factors intensive in specific human capital. The flexibility of educational skills implies their relatively higher substitutability in production. The specificity of experience skills implies complementarity in production. This evidence consequently supports the characteristics ascribed to general and specific human capital of Becker (1975).

Given the elasticity of substitution estimates, the sensitivity to policy considerations affecting the demand for labor by age can be examined. Two specific programs directly affecting labor demand by age are social security and minimum wages. Consider an increase in social security benefits, increasing the opportunity cost of labor and the relative price of older workers. In addition, if employer contributions at a given wage are increased to fund the program, employer costs are increased relatively for older workers, since expected length of service decreases with age.[28]

From the second column, an increase in the relative wage of older workers implies the substitution of the adjacent category, middle–aged workers and physical capital, and a decrease in the demand for younger workers, given the complementarity of specific and general skills. As a consequence, such a policy increases the intensity of the capital-skill aggregate in production.

Minimum wage legislation increases the user cost of younger workers and the relative price with respect to other factors of production. In this case, middle-aged workers and capital are substituted for younger workers, and the demand for older workers decreases. Consequently, the skill aggregate is relatively highly substitutable for general skills, as opposed to specific skills. Increases in the minimum wage consequently lead to increased physical capital and skill intensity in production.

## Conclusion

Technical change augments skill-intensive age groups more rapidly than other, less skill-intensive ages. Substitution possibilities also induce relative increases in demand at fixed wages, as physical capital is relatively more complementary with human capital–intensive ages. These effects are explanatory causes for the observed constancy of relative wages for human capital classifications.

An aggregate of capital and middle-aged workers is accepted, separable from younger and middle-aged workers, while all other mutually exclusive and exhaustive forms are rejected. Decomposing the human capital element in each age group into experience and education, or specific and general skills, it is shown that experience is highly complementary with age and education highly substitutable for age in production.

Finally, increases in social security contributions and minimum wages are shown to lead to increases in the physical capital and skill intensity of production, and to decreases in quantity demands for relatively unskilled younger and older workers in each case.

# 7

# CONCLUSIONS AND
# POLICY IMPLICATIONS

## Employment Composition and Productivity

This research has developed a theoretical structure for the analysis of productivity change. It has explained productivity change as the sum of components attributable to various capital and labor sources. Within the context of the potential existence of a labor subaggregate, other issues have been examined, notably whether various types of human capital inputs can be combined together in production.

Several main conclusions are derived from the productivity decomposition, as examined in Chapters 2 and 3. From the aggregate consideration of productivity change in the U.S. private domestic economy for 1947–1974, the following conclusions are derived.

There has been a role reversal in the relative contributions of total employment, measured as hours worked, and labor skills per hour to the measurement of labor input. Total employment over the 1947–1958 period grew relatively slowly, at 0.37 percent per annum, while labor quality grew at an annual rate of 0.75 percent. Labor quality represents the combined effects of age, sex, class of worker (self-employed or employed), occupation, and education of worker and all interactive effects of these characteristics. During the 1958–1972 period, labor input grew at 2.05 percent per annum, but the rate of employment growth was 1.70 percent and that of labor quality only 0.35 percent. It appears that the relatively large contribution made by labor skills in the period up to 1958 has ended.

108

Within the labor component, the five characteristics used to identify employment can be further examined to determine the sources of the relative decline in labor skills per hour or labor quality. Considering age, where workers are divided into eight groups, the age effect increases labor input by 0.34 percent per year for 1947–1951, but this changes to −0.29 percent for 1971–1974. At an aggregate share of labor in value added of two-thirds, this implies that the shifting age composition towards youth alone decreases output by 0.2 percent per year.

The effect of sex composition, reflecting the continued increase of women in share of total employment, is to reduce labor input. However, the magnitude of the effect changes little over the postwar period, so the collapse of labor quality cannot be attributed to the growth in female employment.

For education, long considered a contributor to economic growth, the results indicate a diminished effect. During the peak period of 1963–1967, education increased labor input by 0.85 percent per year, but by 1971–1974 this had been reduced to 0.67 percent. This contribution depends on two factors. Since more educated people are paid higher wages than less educated people, and since wages are used as reflective of productivity weights, relative employment increases for the educated increase labor input. Second, an additional contribution arises if the relative wage of the educated rises with respect to the less educated.

Freeman (1976) and others have shown that the latter has failed to occur in the 1970s. If relative wages of the less educated are rising, education ultimately could have a negative effect on productivity growth.

Finally, a large negative contributor is occupational composition, which exerts a positive 0.42 percent effect for 1955–1959 and a negative 0.29 percent effect for 1971–1974. The employment composition results may be summarized as follows:

1.  The share of employment growth accounted for by skill composition is decreasing, and its growth rate is decreasing.
2.  Age, education, and occupation composition are the main contributors in the forms of the increasing share of employment by youth, the declining relative wages of the educated, and the shift to unskilled occupations.

There are substantial policy implications of these findings. If extensive skill or total employment is growing at the expense of intensive skill or training, resources should be allocated to placement, counseling, and employment services, with the goal of improving the transitions to employment and between jobs. Upgrading or retraining programs require less relative attention, because the relative return to the economy in increased productivity is not guaranteed.

The education and occupation results confirm declining returns to high levels of education, particularly to relatively skilled jobs in professional and managerial categories. The implication for public retraining programs is to emphasize primary and secondary education, for example, with programs for immigrants or to allocate further resources to existing elementary and high schools. Further, occupational retraining should be focused on relatively unskilled jobs. Professional education should be de-emphasized.

One additional conclusion arises from the employment composition research. It is shown that biases arise from an incorrectly specified functional form for labor input. Adding together growth rates of components leads to upward biases in labor input growth. For statistical agencies or researchers constructing these aggregates, a form that takes into account all the interactions is required. Previous estimates of labor input growth have failed to take this into account.

## Labor Productivity

The procedures on the construction of labor input are used in the examination of labor and total factor productivity growth for the U.S. private domestic economy for 1947–1974. Labor productivity is decomposed into three categories, namely, total factor productivity, capital intensity, and labor quality.

The results, as indicated in Table 4.3 suggest an average increase in labor productivity of 2.61 percent over the period, but with a virtual disappearance to 0.65 percent over the 1971–1974 period. The conclusion is that labor productivity has declined substantially since the early 1960s: from a growth rate of 3.37 percent annually for 1959–1963, the increase in labor productivity declines to 2.66 percent for 1963–1967, 2.13 percent for 1967–1971 and 0.65 percent for 1971–1974.

Over the 1947–1974 period, total factor productivity virtually disappears. For 1959–1963, this index of outputs to inputs increases on average at 1.41 percent per year. By 1971–1974, there is a decrease to −0.13 percent annually. Labor quality exhibits a similar pattern, with virtually a zero increase over 1960–1970. The labor quality effect, defined as the product of the labor share in value added and the growth rate of labor skills, contributes 0.76 percent per year to labor productivity for 1959–1963 and 0.08 percent for 1971–1974.

Finally, labor productivity is shown to depend on the degree of capital intensity in the economy. Greater capital intensity implies that each effective worker is using more plant and equipment, yielding greater output per hour. For 1959–1963, the capital intensity effect, or the capital share multiplied by capital per hour, increases by 1.20 percent, with the 1971–1974 increase amounting to 0.70 percent. The decline in labor productivity is not principally attributable to capital intensity. While this factor on average accounts for 50 percent of productivity growth in labor over the entire period, it actually exceeds total labor productivity change for 1971–1974.

To summarize:

1. Labor productivity growth, at a consistent rate of 2–3 percent annually private domestic economy up to the 1970s, virtually disappears in the 1970s.
2. A collapse in total factor productivity growth occurs in the U.S. in the period after the 1960s. Growth of about 1 percent historically becomes almost zero after this point.
3. Capital intensity growth is reduced, but not to the same extent as total factor productivity or labor quality.

There are several policy implications of the above conclusions. The existence of a productivity crisis is confirmed. The main cause of the productivity slowdown appears to be declines in total factor productivity, alternatively described as the residual or as advances to knowledge. To stimulate this growth requires investment in basic research and development. Moreover, while attempts to spur capital accumulation will ultimately improve labor productivity, stimulation of basic research may yield a greater response.

## Aggregation in Production

Tests of various types of aggregation in production have been reported here. Three alternative two-way groupings are examined. The first is the conventional capital and labor dichotomy, which distinguishes physical or nonhuman inputs from human inputs. The second is a skilled-unskilled classification. The former group includes relatively skilled workers and equipment or machinery. The latter includes unskilled workers and plant. The third categorization involves the distinction between production inputs such as equipment and blue-collar workers and nonproduction inputs of plant and white-collar labor. An alternative division for the last option is that of nonoverhead and overhead inputs.

Tests are performed for this aggregation, and the first two forms are rejected. However, the third combination cannot be rejected by the data. This suggests that the conventional grouping of capital and labor requires re-examination.

Estimates of substitution possibilities in production are also presented. The following results are obtained:

1.  Plant and white-collar workers (or overhead) are complementary. This supports the hypothesis of capital-skill complementarity. Purchases of additional plant impose labor requirements for white-collar employees.
2.  Substitution elasticities between other combinations are all positive but relatively low, the largest being between plant and blue-collar workers.

In particular, the elasticity of substitution between equipment and plant is 1.84, with the same estimate obtaining between equipment and white-collar labor. The elasticity between equipment and blue-collar labor is 0.62, but not significantly different from zero. Consider an investment tax credit, which reduces the user cost, or effective rental price to the owner-operator, of equipment. Hence an investment tax credit would, while increasing equipment demand for a given output level, reduce the demand for plant and white-collar workers. There could also be an increase in demand for blue-collar labor.

## Aggregation of Age Inputs

Further examination of aggregation over age inputs is performed to shed light on various policy initiatives. Minimum wage legislation, although not specifically targeted to an age group or groups, has been argued as reducing job opportunities for younger workers. Also, payroll taxes for social security and unemployment insurance may induce substitution away from those inputs that are relatively expensive.

Production is examined for a four-factor classification. The four components are capital and workers aged 16–24, 25–64, and 65 and above. Capital is found to be aggregable with workers aged 65 and above.

Young workers are shown to be relatively substitutable for capital. The partial elasticity of substitution is 2.73. The cross-price elasticity of demand with respect to a change in the price of capital services is −1.11. Again, an investment tax credit or other policy regime that reduced the user cost of capital would tend to increase the demand for capital but reduce the demand for younger workers. Younger and older workers are complements, with a partial elasticity of substitution of −0.98. Policies designed to create jobs for youth, such as wage subsidies to employers, or targeted youth employment programs will also increase demand for elderly workers at a given output level. However, demand for workers aged 65 and above and capital declines.

More specifically, the cross-price elasticity of demand for capital with respect to a change in the user cost or demand price of labor to an employer is −0.09, but significantly different from zero. A 1 percent decrease in wages for youth would reduce capital demand by about .1 percent. Policies to subsidize youth employment have been extensively examined from the supply side. Relevant considerations include alternative job opportunities for displaced workers. However, estimation of relevant production functions is required in order to obtain measures of displacement for capital and other workers.

## Concluding Remarks

The research has examined aggregation of labor inputs and the construction of measures of labor productivity. In general, poor productivity performance by the U.S. private domestic economy over the 1970s has been chronicled. A particular observation is the decline and almost disappearance of total factor productivity growth, defined as changes in output per unit of an input index. Accompanying these declines in productivity is a decrease in the contribution of certain employment characteristics, notably education and occupation.

Jorgenson and Griliches (1967, 1972) have argued that the observation of total factor productivity is an aberration. Such may arise from aggregation error in the construction of the input index, from unmeasured effects, or from economies of scale or changes in utilization of factors. Controlling for all other factors is difficult. However, using an identical definition of total factor productivity over the 1947–1974 period yields substantial within-period changes. If excluded factors have contributed to the productivity slowdown, they changed substantially during the period.

It remains the case that observed productivity change in the United States has declined substantially. Moreover, this has been associated with shifts in the composition of employment.

# Appendix A

# CROSS-CLASSIFICATION OF LABOR INPUT

**Table A.1.** Within-Industry Labor Input Classification

| | |
|---|---|
| *Age* | 16–17 |
| | 18–24 |
| | 25–34 |
| | 35–44 |
| | 45–54 |
| | 55–64 |
| | 65 and over |
| *Class of Worker* | Wage and salary workers |
| | Self-employed workers (including unpaid family workers) |
| *Educational Attainment* | Elementary school (0–8 years) |
| | High school (1–3 years) |
| | High school (4 years) |
| | College (1–3 years) |
| | College (4 years and above) |
| *Occupation* | Professionals |
| | Farmers and farm managers |
| | Managers |
| | Clerical |
| | Sales |
| | Craftsmen |
| | Operatives |
| | Services (including private household workers) |
| | Farm laborers |
| | Laborers |
| *Sex* | Male |
| | Female |

**Table A.2.** Industrial Classification

| Code | Industry Listing |
|------|------------------|
| 1 | Agriculture, Forestry, and Fisheries |
| | Mining |
| 2 | Metal Mining |
| 3 | Coal Mining |
| 4 | Crude petroleum and natural gas |
| 5 | Mining and quarrying of nonmetallic minerals |
| 6 | Contract Construction |
| | Manufacturing: Nondurable Goods |
| 7 | Food and kindred products |
| 8 | Tobacco manufacturers |
| 9 | Textile mill products |
| 10 | Apparel and other fabricated products |
| 11 | Paper and allied products |
| 12 | Printing, publishing, and allied industries |
| 13 | Chemicals and allied products |
| 14 | Petroleum refining and related industries |
| 15 | Rubber and miscellaneous plastic products |
| 16 | Leather and leather products |
| | Manufacturing: Durable Goods |
| 17 | Lumber and wood products, except furniture |
| 18 | Furniture and fixtures |
| 19 | Stone, clay, and glass products |
| 20 | Primary metal industries |
| 21 | Fabricated metal products |
| 22 | Machinery, except electrical |
| 23 | Electrical machinery |
| | Manufacturing: Durable Goods |
| 24 | Transportation equipment and ordinance, except motor vehicles |
| 25 | Motor vehicles and motor vehicle equipment |
| 26 | Instruments |
| 27 | Miscellaneous manufacturing industries |
| | Transportation |
| 28 | Railroad transportation |
| 29 | Local, suburban, and highway passenger |
| 30 | Motor freight transportation and warehousing |
| 31 | Water transportation |
| 32 | Air transportation |
| 33 | Pipeline transportation |
| 34 | Transportation services |

**Table A.2.**  Industrial Classification (continued)

| Code | Industry Listing |
|------|------------------|
| | Communications |
| 35 | Telephone and telegraph |
| 36 | Radio broadcasting and television |
| | Electric, Gas, and Sanitary Services |
| 37 | Electric light and power |
| | Electric and gas utilities |
| | Gas and steam supply systems |
| 38 | Water supply |
| | Sanitary services |
| | Other utilities |
| | Wholesale and Retail Trade |
| 39 | Wholesale trade |
| 40 | Retail trade |
| | Finance, Insurance, and Real Estate |
| 41 | Banking and credit |
| 42 | Security and commodity brokerage and investment companies |
| 43 | Insurance |
| 44 | Real Estate |
| | Services |
| 45 | Hotels and lodging |
| 46 | Personal services |
| 47 | Private households |
| 48 | Advertising and miscellaneous business services |
| 49 | Auto repair and garages |
| 50 | Miscellaneous repair services |
| 51 | Theatres and motion pictures |
| 52 | Amusement and recreation except motion pictures |
| 53 | Medical services |
| 54 | Legal services |
| 55 | Educational services |
| 56 | Welfare, religious services, and nonprofit organizations |
| 57 | Engineering and architectural services |
| | Accounting and auditing services |
| | Miscellaneous professional and related services |

# Appendix B

# LABOR QUALITY
# CHANGE PROJECTIONS

The model for projection of labor quality commences with a system of difference equations governing the growth of population, with parametric specifications for rates of mortality, fertility, and net immigration. This system in turn is associated with equations for labor force, employment, and total hours projections, given parametric specifications or participation rates and unemployment rates.

Total additions to the population, in the first age group are

$$P(0, j, t) = [1 - \delta(0, j, t)] \sum_{i=i_0}^{i_1} \alpha(i, 2, t) P(i, 2, t)$$
$$+ \phi(0, j, t) \tag{B.1}$$

where $P(i, j, t)$ is the number of persons in the population of age $i$ and of sex $j$ at time $t$. The mortality rate for persons in the $i$th age and $j$th sex cohort at time $t$ is $\delta(i, j, t)$, and the number of net immigrants in the same cohort at time $t$ is $\phi(i, j, t)$. The number of births in each year is the number of women in the childbearing span $[i_0, i_1]$ multiplied by the birth rate $\alpha(i, 2, t)$ for $i \in [i_0, i_1]$. In addition, the initial condition, or the population at time zero $P(i, j, 0)$ is given. The number of surviving additions to the population is consequently the number of births adjusted by the infant mortality rate, in addition to the number of immigrants.

The number of persons in the $i$th age group, $i > 0$, is the number of surviving individuals for the previous age group in the previous year, in addition to net immigrants in the cohort. This relation is

$$P(i, j, t) = [1 - \delta(i, j, t)]P(i-1, j, t-1) + \phi(i, j, t) \qquad \text{(B.2)}$$

at time $t$. This yields a set of population projections by age and sex, contingent on the parametric selection of birth and death rates and the number of net immigrants.

The labor force in each cohort is defined as the participation rate multiplied by the population in the cohort. Consequently,

$$L(i, j, k, t) = \lambda(i, j, k, t)P(i, j, t) \qquad \text{(B.3)}$$

where $L(i, j, k, t)$ is the labor force total of persons with sex $i$, age $j$, and educational attainment $k$ at time $t$, and $\lambda(i, j, k, t)$ is the labor force participation rate for the same cohort. Each sex-age cohort has an educational classification, allowing the construction of such projections. Finally, total hours worked in each cohort can be represented as

$$H(i, j, k, t) = 1 - \beta(i, j, k, t)\gamma(i, j, k, t)L(i, j, k, t) \qquad \text{(B.4)}$$

where $\beta(i, j, k, t)$ and $\gamma(i, j, k, t)$ are respectively the unemployment rates and the hours worked per person in cohorts $i$, $j$, $k$ and $H(i, j, k, t)$ is the total hours worked at time $t$.

By specifying the cohort wage $W(i, j, k, t)$, a Törnqvist index growth rate for labor input is

$$\Delta \ln D(t) = \sum_{i-1}^{I} \sum_{j-1}^{J} \sum_{k-1}^{K} v(i, j, k, t)\, \Delta \ln H(i, j, k, t) \qquad \text{(B.5)}$$

where $v(i, j, k, t)$ is the relative share of that factor in total compensation. The change in an unweighted manhours index is

$$\Delta \ln M(t) = \Delta \ln \sum_{i-1}^{I} \sum_{j-1}^{J} \sum_{k-1}^{K} H(i, j, k, t)$$

from whence the quality index growth is defined

$$\Delta \ln Q(t) = \Delta \ln D(t) - \Delta \ln M(t)$$

at time $t$.

The data used in the model are as follows:

i.  Initial population
    A classification of the population by sex and age, from the 1970 census count.
ii.  Birth rates
    The Census of Population projections series C, assuming a fertility rate of 2.775 children born per woman in a childbearing span from age 14 to age 49. This is combined with the census distribution of births over the span, to yield a cohort birth rate.
iii.  Death rates
    The rates used are the survival rates by sex and age published by the Census Bureau.
iv.  Immigration levels
    The rates are as in iii.
v.  Labor force participation rates
    The Bureau of Labor Statistics (BLS) projects the labor force by sex, age, and education. These results yield an implicit series of participation rates.
vi.  Unemployment rates
    The actual 1972 rates by sex, age, and education from the BLS were held constant to the year 2000.
vii.  Hours
    Total hours, the product of weeks paid per year and hours worked per week paid, were held constant to the year 2000 at the 1972 level.
viii.  Wages
    Relative wages were held constant at the 1972 level. This assumes perfect substitutability between cohorts.

The empirical results are summarized in Table B.1. It is noted that labor quality decreases monotonically to the year 2000. There are several causal factors accounting for this phenomenon:

1.  The educational distribution of the BLS converges by 1985, and at lower age cohorts, no shifts are projected in the distribution.

2.  The projected birth rates are based on a fertility rate of 2.775, as opposed to lower values observed in the 1970s. These values increase quality, as there would be lower proportions of workers under 35 in the year 2000.

3.  An increase in the proportion of women among employed persons is projected.

**Table B.1.**  Projections of Labor Quality, 1972–2000, Indexes, 1983 = 1.000

| Year | Labor Input | Total Hours | Quality |
|------|-------------|-------------|---------|
| 1972 | .914 | .821 | 1.113 |
| 1973 | .922 | .839 | 1.098 |
| 1974 | .929 | .858 | 1.084 |
| 1975 | .936 | .876 | 1.069 |
| 1976 | .945 | .893 | 1.059 |
| 1977 | .954 | .909 | 1.049 |
| 1978 | .962 | .926 | 1.039 |
| 1979 | .970 | .942 | 1.030 |
| 1980 | .978 | .959 | 1.020 |
| 1981 | .987 | .973 | 1.014 |
| 1982 | .993 | .986 | 1.007 |
| 1983 | 1.000 | 1.000 | 1.000 |
| 1984 | 1.007 | 1.014 | .993 |
| 1985 | 1.013 | 1.027 | .986 |
| 1986 | 1.023 | 1.043 | .981 |
| 1987 | 1.033 | 1.058 | .977 |
| 1988 | 1.043 | 1.073 | .972 |
| 1989 | 1.052 | 1.088 | .967 |
| 1990 | 1.062 | 1.103 | .962 |
| 1991 | 1.074 | 1.122 | .957 |
| 1992 | 1.087 | 1.142 | .952 |
| 1993 | 1.098 | 1.161 | .946 |
| 1994 | 1.110 | 1.180 | .941 |
| 1995 | 1.122 | 1.200 | .935 |
| 1996 | 1.133 | 1.219 | .930 |
| 1997 | 1.144 | 1.238 | .924 |
| 1998 | 1.155 | 1.258 | .918 |
| 1999 | 1.166 | 1.277 | .913 |
| 2000 | 1.176 | 1.296 | .907 |

# NOTES

## 2. The Measurement of Labor Input

1. This repackaging of a commodity aggregate, with the implied adjustment in price and quantity, is considered in Fisher and Shell (1971) and in Griliches (1971).

2. The connection between this type of index and exact functional forms for the underlying aggregates is derived in Diewert (1976, 1980).

3. Optimal properties of Divisia index numbers in continuous time are derived in Richter (1966). The original derivation is in Divisia (1926). An index number problem arises in the application to any discrete data.

4. An alternative starting point in the aggregation of labor inputs is the production function. The function aggregating labor and non-labor inputs is assumed separable between these two groups, and the labor subaggregate assumed homogeneous. Given these assumptions, the associated indirect function possesses the same properties. The cost function approach has been applied to labor input aggregation by Waldorf (1973).

5. An exact approximation error of this form is derived by Star and Hall (1974). An alternative specification is a moving geometric mean of the arithmetic and geometric mean shares. Both these forms are proposed by Theil (1967, 1973). Diewert (1976) proposes the Fisher ideal index as an alternative form. See also Lau (1979).

6. A detailed discussion of differences in procedure and measurement between the household and establishment surveys is contained in Green (1969).

7. A definition of multiple job holder coverage is contained in BLS *Special Labor Force Report* (*SLFR*) 139 (1972). Among U.S. civilian persons engaged in the 1950–1971 period, multiple job holders represented between

4.5 and 5.5 percent of the total, according to household data. Of the multiple job holders, 90 percent work at exactly two jobs.

8. For a discussion of the bias introduced in labor input series by failure to correct for multiple job holders, see Green (1969).

9. For series on full- and part-time wage and salary workers, see the *Survey of Current Business (SCB)*, July national income issues, Table 6.1. Similar data on employment in production are contained in Table 6.3.

10. No person is classified as a multiple job holder who has a work activity as an unpaid family worker [*SLFR*, 139 (1972), p. 38], and only wage and salary workers are counted among unpaid absentees. This provides the justification for adding household unpaid family workers to establishment employment. Such a procedure is adopted by Christensen and Jorgenson (1973, p. 285), Jorgenson and Griliches (1972, p. 77), and Kendrick (1973).

11. Some evidence on the extent and composition of unpaid absenteeism is presented in Denison (1974, Table C-8).

12. Both household and establishment series define full-time or part-time status according to whether a person worked more or fewer than 35 hours during a survey week.

13. The addition of persons engaged in Alaska and Hawaii resulted in an increase of 0.4 percent in U.S. private domestic employment in 1960 (from *SCB* July 1961, p. 5).

14. See *SLFR* 76 (1967), Table A-1, and *SLFR* 91 (1968), Table A-2.

15. The effect of the reclassification in 1966 was to reduce the number of self-employed persons from 6.1 million to 5.3 million as in *SLFR* 76 (1967), Table A-1, and *SLFR* 91 (1968), Table A-2. This reconciles a large portion of the difference in the self-employment count between establishment and household surveys, given that the former consistently classifies corporate officers as employees.

16. Such statistical matches are considered in Budd (1972) and Okner (1972). Other statistical matches in labor classifications are performed by Barger (1971), Gollop (1974), and Star (1974).

17. Proofs of existence and uniqueness of the solution to the transactions form of the procedure are derived in Bacharach (1970).

18. An iteration for the algorithm is defined as one pass, with associated premultiplier computations, through all constraint arrays.

19. For the year 1947, the converged 1950 value is used as the initialization. The 1948 and 1949 starting values are subsequently constructed by interpolating between 1947 and 1950. For 1972, the converged 1970 value is used as the initialization, with 1971 initialized from converged values for 1970 and 1972.

20. It is assumed that all multiple job holders possess exactly two jobs, although this is not the case for 10 percent of the total. However, published data are available only for primary and secondary employment.

21.   See, for example, the *Detailed Characteristics Final Report PC(1), D1*, 1970 Census, Appendix B.

22.   See *Detailed Characteristics*, Appendix B.

23.   These data represent weekly total hours in production, as opposed to annual hours.

24.   See *SLFR* 139 (1972), p. 38.

25.   The maximum likelihood properties of multinomial estimation are derived in Rao (1973). The algorithm used to determine the local maximum is the Fletcher-Powell method.

26.   Data on earnings are also used in the MML procedure and are converted to equivalent wage and salary form by proportional adjustment.

27.   See *NIPA Historical Summary*, 1966, ix. These include social security, federal and state unemployment insurance, railroad retirement unemployment insurance, and government retirement insurance. Nonstatutory contributions include employer payments on behalf of employees to private pension, health, unemployment and welfare funds, compensation for injuries, directors' fees, and pay of the military reserve.

28.   An alternative procedure is to compute the wage residually by dividing earnings of self-employed persons less the value of capital services, with an imputed return, by hours worked. Christensen (1971) discusses both alternatives.

## 3.   Sources of Quality Change

1.   Weak separability of labor and nonlabor inputs, together with homotheticity of the direct production function, implies a separable wage aggregate within the dual cost function. This starting point is used by Waldorf (1973) in construction estimates of labor quality.

2.   See Christensen, Jorgenson, and Lau (1971, 1973).

3.   This translog growth rate is derived by Star and Hall (1974), with the approximation error for arithmetic share weighting of discrete data. The relation between the procedure and translog functions in homogeneous form is derived by Diewert (1976, 1980).

4.   This partial index is developed and applied to labor input measurement by Barger (1971). The structure is applied to the explanation of labor input growth in aggregate U.S. manufacturing, 1948–1966.

5.   The aggregation bias in measuring labor input by total hours is noted in Jorgenson and Griliches (1967, 1972). If $q_j > 0$, labor input is understated, and the difference between output growth and aggregate input growth, total factor productivity, is biased upward.

6.   A version of this noninteractive index is applied to labor input measurement by Denison (1974), for the U.S. business sector, 1929–1969. The

form used contains four factors: class of worker, sex, age, and education. A sex-age interaction is permitted, but others are restricted to zero.

7. Labor factors are added in a specified order to a total hours index. Since sex is the first factor included, the measure is the sex effect. The estimate exceeds that in Table 3.3, but labor is defined by employment as opposed to total hours worked.

8. Denison constructs imputed noncorporate income using a scale factor based on employee wages and corporate after-tax returns applied to labor and capital, respectively.

9. The educational index weights distributions of employment by earnings relatives, assuming perfect substitutability among educational levels.

10. In Barger (1971) an aggregate for U.S. manufacturing by sex, age, and education is reduced from 1948–1960 to 1960–1966. Waldorf (1973), using an occupational classification for U.S. manufacturing, obtains a decrease in labor quality from 1952–1960 to 1960–1967.

## 4. Labor Skills and Productivity Measurement

1. In the initial research, Jorgenson and Griliches (1967) obtained a growth rate of total factor productivity for the U.S. for 1939–1960 of 0.1 percent, but in later (1972) work, this estimate was revised upwards to over 1 percent.

2. The large increase in relative prices of fuels in 1973–1974 may not be completely adjusted to during the sample period. There is evidence that these increases in relative prices also occurred to a less marked extent prior to 1973–1974. See also Berndt and Khaled (1979).

3. See Griliches (1970) and Christensen and Jorgenson (1973).

4. The term skilled in this context may be a misnomer. The actual classification used is taken from the BLS establishment survey and divides workers into production and nonproduction. The latter are deemed skilled.

5. These conclusions are obtained by Christensen (1971), Kuznets (1971), and Denison (1974).

6. A two-stage procedure involving the aggregation of labor inputs $z(x_1, \ldots, x_M)$ and $k(x_{M+1}, \ldots, x_N)$ separately, and combining the $z$ and $k$ subaggregates to form value added, is *consistent in aggregation* if the same index number is obtained from $f(x_1, \ldots, x_M, x_{M+1}, \ldots, x_N)$. This terminology is developed in Vartia (1976), and Diewert (1978) shows that conditions (4.2) are required to derive these results. Blackorby and Primont (1979) derive the conditions for consistency in aggregation from functional analysis.

7. The formulation of a value added index requires that separability obtain between the labor and capital service inputs $x_1, \ldots, x_N$ and inputs of

raw materials and energy $x_{N+1}, \ldots, x_p$ to the extent that these are excluded from the list of capital inputs (Arrow 1974). If consistency in aggregation also obtains for gross production $y_G = y_G(y(x_1, \ldots, x_N), x_{N+1}, \ldots, x_P)$ then little information is lost in using the value added index $y$ as a first stage in constructing $y_G$. This requires only that $y_G$ satisfy (2). This is a consequence of the work by Diewert (1978).

8.    Under conditions (4.2), a dual approach to the measurement of labor productivity is possible. The cost function per unit of value added $y$ is $c(p)$, where $p = (p_1, \ldots, p_M)$, obeying $f(x) = 1/\max\{c(p):p \cdot x = 1, p \geq 0\}$ where $x = (x_1, \ldots, x_N)$. If both $f(x)$ and $c(p)$ attain their maxima, $f(x)c(p)$ equals current value added. Since this is fixed, $df(x)c(p)$ is $d$ times value added, requiring $d^* = 1/d$ as the diminution of total cost to be applied to the unit cost function. Since the labor subaggregate satisfies (4.2), $z(x^M) = q(x^M)h = 1/\max\{w_z(p^M):p^N \cdot x^M = 1, p^M \geq 0\}$ where $x^M = (x_1, \ldots, x_M)$ and $p^M = (p_1, \ldots, p_M)$ and $w_z$ is the wage of a unit of labor. By duality, $w_z(p^M)$ satisfies conditions (4.2). Let $wh$ be total labor cost, where $w$ is the average hourly wage, a scalar. Then $w_z(p^M) = w_z(p^M) = w_z(p^M/w)w = q^*(p^M)w$, but $z(x^N)w_z(p^N) = wh$, implying $q^* = 1/q$. If $w_k(p^{N-M})$ is the rental price of capital services, where $p^{N-M} = (p_{M+1}, \ldots, p_N)$, then $c^*(p) = d^{-1}c(w_z/q, w_k)$ where $c^*$ is $c/d$. Since the cost function is derived from the production function, it is differentiable even if the latter is not, yielding

$$\frac{\partial \ln c^*(p)}{\partial t} = \frac{-\partial \ln d}{\partial t} + s_z \left[ \frac{\partial \ln w_z}{\partial t} - \frac{\partial \ln q}{\partial t} \right] + s_k \frac{\partial \ln w_k}{\partial t}$$

analogous to (4.5).

9.    The general form contains $k$ characteristics selected from $k$, so there are $(K-k)!$ of these. If factors are renumbered so that only the first $k$ are considered,

$$x(i_1, \ldots, i_k) = \sum_{i_{k+1}-1}^{I_{k+1}} \cdots \cdots \sum_{i_k-1}^{I_k} x(i_1, \ldots, i_k)$$

and information on the last $(K-k)$ characteristics is suppressed. The wage for each of these

$$\prod_{j-1}^{k} I_j \text{ labor types is } p(i_1, \ldots, i_k) = C(i_1, \ldots, i_k)/x(i_1, \ldots, i_k)$$

where

$$C(i_1, \ldots, i_k) = \sum_{i_{k+1}-1}^{I_{k-1}} \cdots \sum_{i_k-1}^{I_k} p(i_1, \ldots, i_k)x(i_1, \ldots, i_k)$$

is the labor compensation of workers with characteristics $i_1, \ldots, i_k$.

10.    If gross investment for a given durable good type is $INV_t$ in year $t$, and time is measured in discrete units and $k_0$ is a benchmark or initial period capital stock, with $t = 0, \ldots, T$ then

$$k_t = (1 - \delta)^t k_0 + \sum_{s=0}^{t} (1 - \delta)^s INV_{t-s}$$

is the capital stock at time $t$, where $\delta$ is a constant rate of depreciation.

11.    The translog form satisfies the consistency in aggregation condition only approximately, but the errors are shown to be negligible. As a practical application in measuring labor productivity, suppose the production function is re-expressed $y_G = f(dy(x_1, \ldots, x_M, x_{M+1}, \ldots, x_N), x_{N+1}, \ldots, x_p)$ where $z(x_1, \ldots, x_M)$ groups labor inputs, $k(x_{M+1}, \ldots, x_N)$ groups capital inputs, and $m(x_{N+1}, \ldots, x_p)$ groups intermediate inputs, and $y_G$ represents gross output. Consistency in aggregation implies that the y index number in this form is identical to that obtained by $f(dy, x_{N+1}, \ldots, x_p)$ where $y(x_1, \ldots, x_k)$ is value added.

12.    For the four factor case, the combined quality effect is for the first two factors

$$\Delta \ln q^*(1, 2) = \sum_{i_1=1}^{I_1} \sum_{i_2=1}^{I_2} v(i_1, i_2) \Delta \ln x(i_1, i_2) - \Delta \ln h$$

where the $v(i_1, i_2)$ are constructed as two-year moving averages of shares. By analogy with the analysis of variance, the first-order interactive effect between the first two factors is $\Delta \ln b(1, 2) = \Delta \ln q(1, 2) - \Delta \ln q(1) - \Delta \ln q(2)$. The contribution of the interaction to productivity growth is $v_z \Delta \ln b(1, 2)$. Higher order interactions are treated analogously.

13.    Imputed labor compensation from this procedure is subtracted from total noncorporate income, yielding an estimate of capital income in the noncorporate sector. If this is lower than the after tax return on corporate capital, resources might be more productively used in the corporate sector if no psychic income is earned in entrepreneurship.

14.    An equivalent approach to that used here is taken by Medoff (1978) in estimating substitution between labor inputs by sex. Griliches (1977) points out that corrections for discrimination should be based on an explicit model. If not, the typically large residual, which may reflect other considerations, is erroneously attached to discrimination.

## 5.    Aggregation of Inputs and Technical Change

1.    Such truncation of inputs through aggregation to a group of needs is discussed in Lancaster (1966) and Rosen (1974).

2. The translog approximation to an arbitrary production function is developed in Christensen, Jorgenson, and Lau (1971, 1973).

3. For a discussion, see Lau (1974). The method proposed is a Cholesky factorization of the Hessian matrix, involving a diagonalization of the given matrix. Convexity obtains if all entries on the principal diagonal are positive. An alternative and equivalent method of verification is the computation of all principal minors of (5.7), which are positive for convexity.

4. The restrictions on a multiple input production function implied by factor augmentation are derived by Burmeister and Dobell (1969).

5. This hypothesis has been advanced by Boddy and Gort (1971) as an explanatory factor for observed increases in the relative quantities of equipment to plant over time. Empirical evidence supporting increased equipment intensity is presented in Jorgenson and Griliches (1972) and Kendrick (1973) for U.S. 1947–1966 data.

6. Localized technical progress is considered by Atkinson and Stiglitz (1969).

7. For a discussion, see Welch (1970) and Dougherty (1972). This is hypothesized as another causal factor for increasing quantity ratios of skilled to unskilled labor, associated with constant relative wages.

8. Such adaptive and innovative advantages are accorded skilled labor by Nelson and Phelps (1966).

9. This restriction on pairwise elasticities of substitution is derived in Berndt and Christensen (1973b).

10. See Allen (1938). At points other than [1], the elasticity of substitution is $\sigma_{ij} = (v_i v_j + \beta_{ij})/v_i v_j$.

11. For a discussion of capital aggregation see Fisher (1969). Heterogeneous capital goods can be aggregated if the ratio of marginal products of any two of the goods is constant, or if these goods are used in fixed proportions in production.

12. For a more general specification, a production aggregate can be tested as including energy inputs and intermediate goods used in process.

13. Such skill aggregates for labor inputs are considered by Welch (1969). A similar procedure using principal components is applied by Mitchell (1969).

14. The hypothesis of relative equipment-labor substitutability is advanced by Boddy and Gort (1971) as an explanatory factor for increased relative quantities of equipment to plant over time. If the price of labor increases relative to the prices of equipment and plant, the equipment intensity of production will increase. Empirical evidence supporting increased equipment intensity is presented in Jorgenson and Griliches (1972) and Kendrick (1973) for U.S. 1947–1966 data.

15. This hypothesis is proposed by Griliches (1969) and Welch (1970)

as a factor explaining an observed constancy in the relative wage of skilled as opposed to unskilled workers, despite a relative increase in the employment of the former. This constancy has been observed in private rates of return to schooling for the U.S. by Becker (1975) for 1939–1959 and by Freeman (1976) for 1959–1972. Relative earnings ratios by age and education for the U.S. in the two decades following World War II are shown to be constant in Amacher and Freeman (1973) and Griliches (1970).

16.    See Bowles (1967) and Dougherty and Selowsky (1973). In calculating occupational needs, the method of weighting by relative wages assumes perfect substitutability by labor cohort.

17.    The manpower requirements approach assumes zero substitutability within labor. Perfect complementarity between skills implies that input-output arrays can be used to project occupational demands. Low substitutability or complementarity between labor inputs is proposed by Freeman (1974) and Tinbergen (1975).

18.    See Boddy and Gort (1971).

19.    Evidence on differing distributed lag structures for plant and equipment, associated with differing adjustment costs, is presented in Hall and Jorgenson (1971). Putty-clay specifications, and the impact on the demand for capital goods, yield similar conclusions in Bischoff (1969).

20.    See Sato (1967) in the context of an imposed capital aggregate.

21.    The blue-collar classification includes craftsmen, operatives, service workers, private household workers, farm laborers, and laborers. The white-collar classification includes professionals, managers, farmers and farm managers, and clerical and sales workers.

22.    Such a model has been tested, with homogeneity and a Hicks augmentation form as maintained hypotheses, by Berndt and Christensen (1974).

23.    Dougherty (1972) obtains significant differentials in augmentation rates for more disaggregate occupational data. Normalizing with operatives at zero augmentation, the rate for professionals is 1.31 percent, and that for laborers is −0.48 percent. However, these results cannot identify changes in substitution possibilities or the level of technology as causal factors.

24.    Sato (1967) tests equality of plant and equipment augmentation factors and is unable to reject the hypothesis of relative equipment augmentation. The two-level CES form used contains equipment, plant, and labor, with hypothesis testing applied to the capital subaggregate. Equipment is augmented more rapidly than plant at an annual rate of .025.

25.    See Freeman (1974) where for educational and age classifications from household data, increasing relative quantities of skilled labor are associated with an increase in the relative price of unskilled labor for the U.S. 1968–1972.

26.  The periods 1917–1919 and 1940–1947 are excluded from the sample. In addition, evidence of lower substitutability between plant and equipment is indicated by the inclusion of labor in the system, which reduces the elasticity estimates.

27.  For an educational classification and an international cross-section, Bowles (1970) obtains estimates of between 6.4 and 12.0. Psacharopoulos and Hinchliffe (1972), with a similar series, obtain a minimum estimate of 2.2. Dougherty (1972), using cross-section state data for the U.S. census, fits a CES aggregate of educational inputs, with an estimate of 9.0. With a similar data base, Welch (1970) presents estimates between 1.4 and 2.8.

28.  The economic implications of the investment tax credit are considered by Hall and Jorgenson (1971) in their study of its effect on the demand for durable goods.

## 6.  Human Capital and Vintage Effects

1.  See Brennan, Taft and Schupack (1967) for a comprehensive discussion of the effects of age in production. The specific problems of older workers are considered in Brittain (1972) and Feldstein (1974), particularly in the context of social security legislation.

2.  In particular, evidence from results of minimum wage legislation suggests capital–young worker substitutability as the minimum wage increases, as in Kaun (1965). Such legislation and its effect on the demand for young workers has been considered by Adie (1973) and Moore (1971).

3.  See Becker (1975).

4.  The relevant measure of the flow of human capital services is from the stock at a given age. An optimal accumulation program implies that this peak is attained prior to the earnings peak. See Ben-Porath (1967).

5.  For a derivation of the translog approximation see Christensen, Jorgenson, and Lau (1973).

6.  This implies the parametric restrictions $\Sigma_{i-1}^{4}\alpha_i = -1$ and $\Sigma_{j-1}^{4}\beta_{ij} = 0, i = 1 \ldots 4$.

7.  For a derivation of general restrictions on the forms in a multi-factor context, see Burmeister and Dobell (1969).

8.  Becker (1975) and Griliches (1970), using data from the U.S. census, provide evidence of a nondecreasing private rate of return to education, despite increasing relative quantities of educated persons, for both high school and college graduates, for 1939–1959. Freeman (1974) presents evidence suggesting a decrease in the return to human capital as the stock accumulates, but constancy in the private return to college education is obtained for the 1959–1972 period.

9. See Amacher and Freeman (1973), where constancy of relative wages by age and education obtains for the U.S. from 1946 to 1970.

10. This hypothesis is proposed by Welch (1970).

11. These relative advantages in adaptation and innovation are proposed by Nelson and Phelps (1966).

12. Localized technical progress of this form is considered in Atkinson and Stiglitz (1969).

13. Such relative augmentation rates have been applied to multifactor labor input specifications by Dougherty (1972). The augmentation rate associated with a given factor is arbitrarily normalized at zero, and relative augmentation with respect to the reference group is indicated by a positive differential.

14. Further restrictions can also be tested, notably equality between pairs of augmentation rates and equality for groups of three factors, one of which is physical capital services.

15. This parameterization can also be expressed in terms of $\rho_{ij} = \rho_{ij} a_j$ where $\rho_{ij} = (\sigma_{ij} - 1)\alpha_i$ is the compensated price elasticity of demand with the origin translated to the point unity, for factor $j$ with respect to a change in the price of factor $i$.

16. Additively separable aggregates can exist without mutually exclusive groupings of inputs. The tests considered are examined to determine conditions under which truncation of the input listing is permissible.

17. For a discussion of such skill combinations among labor inputs see Welch (1969). In the model considered there, a large number of educational groups can be represented by linear combinations of one unskilled and two skilled categories of labor.

18. For a discussion of capital-skill complementarity, see Griliches (1969) and Welch (1970). The hypothesis is advanced as an alternative explanation for the observation of constant relative wages by skill, accompanied by increasing relative quantities of skilled labor.

19. This is a consequence of the relative similarity in skill of adjacent cohorts. For discussion, see Dougherty (1971).

20. See Bowles (1967) and Dougherty and Selowsky (1973) for human capital aggregation models where this high substitutability is maintained.

21. Monotonicity requires that the function be decreasing in inputs. Locally, this requires $-\alpha_i \geq 0$, $i = 1 \ldots 4$ at the point [0]. Convexity requires positive definiteness of the associated Hessian matrix, testable locally for the translog form by the diagonalization of a matrix with typical element

$$\beta_{ij} + \alpha_i \alpha_j \qquad i \neq j$$

$$\beta_{ii} + \alpha_i(\alpha_i - 1) \qquad i = j, \, i, j = 1 \ldots 4$$

and testing against significant negativity of one diagonal entry in the resulting matrix. These tests are derived by Lau (1974).

Test statistics are constructed by computing the ratio of the parameter estimates for $\alpha_i$ and the diagonal elements $\delta_{ii}$ to the associated standard error. These statistics are distributed asymptotically as the standard normal variate. The statistics are:

$$-\alpha_K \geq 0 \quad 65.68 \quad \delta_{KK} \geq 0 \quad 12.97$$

$$-\alpha_Y \geq 0 \quad 47.10 \quad \delta_{YY} \geq 0 \quad -2.60$$

$$-\alpha_M \geq 0 \quad 119.94 \quad \delta_{MM} \geq 0 \quad 12.66$$

$$-\alpha_S \geq 0 \quad 70.95 \quad \delta_{SS} \geq 0 \quad 7.89$$

for monotonicity and convexity. At a significance level of .001 for each test statistic, the critical value is $-3.09$, implying that the function is locally convex and monotone at .008 within the upper bound assigned for testing significance.

22.    These results are similar to those of Dougherty (1972), where relative augmentation differentials for an occupational classification are estimated. The relative differential between professionals and operatives is 1.31 percent per year, and the rate decreases with a narrowing of skill differentials.

23.    The homogeneous translog form is used with labor services for production and nonproduction workers and capital.

24.    In both cases, aggregates of relatively less educated workers can be constructed.

25.    This supports other evidence using educational data from Griliches (1969), Welch (1970), and Psacharopoulos and Hinchliffe (1972).

26.    Bowles (1970) obtains estimates of between 6.4 and 12.0 for education cohorts. Psacharopoulos and Hinchliffe (1972) obtain a minimum estimate of 2.2, also for an educational classification. Further education results are presented by Dougherty (1972), where, among other results, a CES aggregate of educational inputs yields a result of 9.0, and by Welch (1970), where the result is between 1.4 and 2.8. For occupation, Berndt and Christensen (1974) obtain 7.78, and a CES aggregate yields 4.8 in Dougherty (1972, p. 1112).

27.    See Freeman (1974) and Tinbergen (1975).

28.    This also obtains for such fixed employment costs as health and pension plans where insurance pooling increases the relative benefits of older workers. These programs consequently increase the relative user cost of older workers.

# REFERENCES

Adie, D.K. 1973. Teen-Age Unemployment and Real Federal Minimum Wages. *Journal of Political Economy* 81: 435–442.

Allen, R.C., and Diewert, W.E. 1981. Direct Versus Implicit Index Number Formulae and Some Bounds for Superlative Index Number Formulae. *Review of Economics and Statistics, forthcoming.*

Allen, R.G.D. 1938. *Mathematical Analysis for Economists*. London: Macmillan.

Amacher, F., and Freeman, R.B. 1973. Young Labor Market Entrants: An Overview of Supply and Demand 1950–1970. Cambridge, Mass.: MIT Center for Policy Alternatives.

Arrow, K.J. 1974. The Measurement of Real Value Added. In *Nations and Households in Economic Growth: Essays in Honor of Moses Abramovitz*, P.A. David and N.W. Reder, eds. New York: Academic Press, pp. 3–19.

Atkinson, A.B., and Stiglitz, J.E. 1969. A New View of Technological Change. *Economic Journal* 79: 573–579.

Bacharach, M. 1965. Estimating Non-Negative Matrices from Marginal Data. *International Economic Review* 6: 294–310.

—— 1970. *Biproportional Matrices*. Cambridge, England: Cambridge University Press.

Barger, W.J. 1971. *The Measurement of Labor Input: U.S. Manufacturing Industries 1948–1966*, unpublished Ph.D. dissertation. Harvard University.

Becker, G.S. 1975. *Human Capital*. 2nd. ed. New York: National Bureau of Economic Research.

Ben-Porath, Y. 1967. The Production of Human Capital and the Life Cycle of Earnings. *Journal of Political Economy* 75: 352–365.

Berndt, E.R., and Christensen, L.R. 1973a. The Translog Function and the Substitution of Equipment, Structures and Labor in U.S. Manufacturing, 1929–68. *Journal of Econometrics* 1: 62–81.

—— 1973b. The Internal Structure of Functional Relationships: Separability, Substitution and Aggregation. *Review of Economic Studies* 40: 403–410.

—— 1974. Testing for the Existence of a Consistent Aggregate Index of Labor Inputs. *American Economic Review* 64: 391–404.

Berndt, E.R., and Khaled, M. 1979. Parametric Productivity Measurement and Choice Among Flexible Functional Forms. *Journal of Political Economy* 87: 1220–1245.

Bischoff, C. 1969. Hypothesis Testing and the Demand for Capital Goods. *Review of Economics and Statistics* 51: 354–368.

Blackorby, C. and Primont, D. 1979. "Consistency in Aggregation," University of British Columbia, Department of Economics, Discussion paper.

——; and Russell, R.R. 1978. *Duality, Separability and Functional Structure: Theory and Economic Applications.* New York: Elsevier North Holland.

Boddy, R., and Gort, M. 1971. The Substitution of Capital for Capital. *Review of Economics and Statistics* 53: 179–189.

Bowles, S.S. 1967. Efficient Allocation of Resources in Education. *Quarterly Journal of Economics* 87: 189–219.

—— 1970. Aggregation of Labor Inputs in the Economics of Growth and Planning: Experiments with a Two-Level CES Function. *Journal of Political Economy* 78: 68–81.

Brennan, M.; Taft, P.; and Schupack, M. 1967. *The Economics of Age.* New York: Norton.

Brittain, J. 1972. *The Payroll Tax for Social Security.* Washingtion, D.C.: Brookings Institution.

Brown, C., and Medoff, J. 1978. Trade Unions in the Production Process. *Journal of Political Economy* 86: 355–378.

Budd, E.C. 1972. The Creation of a Micordata File for Estimating the Size Distribution of Income. *Annals of Social and Economic Measurement* 1: 317–333.

Burmeister, E., and Dobell, A.R. 1969. Disembodied Technological Change with Several Factors. *Journal of Economic Theory* 1: 1–8.

Chinloy, P.T. 1980a. Sources of Quality Change in Labor Input. *American Economic Review* 70: 108–119.

—— 1980b. Age Substitution, Social Security and Production. Discussion Paper 79-35 (revised July 1980), Department of Economics, University of British Columbia.

Christensen, L.R. 1971. Entrepreneurial Income: How Does it Measure Up? *American Economic Review* 61: 575–585.

Christensen, L.R., and Jorgenson, D.W. 1973. Measuring Economic Performance in the Private Sector. *The Measurement of Social and Economic Performance,* M. Moss, ed. New York: National Bureau of Economic Research, pp. 233–351.

Christensen, L.R.; Jorgensen, D.W.; and Lau, L.J. 1971. Conjugate Duality and the Transcendental Logarithmic Production Function. *Econometrica* 39: 255–256.

———. 1973. Transcendental Logarithmic Production Frontiers. *Review of Economics and Statistics* 55: 28–45.

Denison, E.F. 1974. *Accounting for United States Economic Growth, 1929–1969.* Washington, D.C.: Brookings Institution.

Diewert, W.E. 1976. Exact and Superlative Index Numbers. *Journal of Econometrics* 4: 115–145.

——— 1978. Superlative Index Numbers and Consistency in Aggregation. *Econometrica* 46: 883–900.

——— 1980. Aggregation Problems in the Measurement of Capital. *The Measurement of Capital,* D. Usher, ed. New York: National Bureau of Economic Research.

Divisia, F. 1926. *Economique Rationelle,* Paris: Dunod.

Dougherty, C.R.S. 1971. Optimal Allocation of Investment in Education. *Studies in Development Planning,* H.B. Chenery, ed. Cambridge, Mass.: Harvard University Press.

——— 1972. Estimates of Labor Aggregation Functions. *Journal of Political Economy* 80: 1101–1119.

Dougherty, C.R.S., and Selowsky, M. 1973. Measuring the Effects of the Misallocation of Labor. *Review of Economics and Statistics* 55: 376–380.

Feldstein, M.S. 1974. Social Security, Induced Retirement and Aggregate Capital Accumulation. *Journal of Political Economy* 82: 905–926.

Fisher, F.M. 1965. Embodied Technical Change and the Existence of an Aggregate Capital Stock. *Review of Economic Studies* 32: 263–288.

——— 1969. The Existence of Aggregate Production Functions. *Econometrica* 37: 553–577.

Fisher, F.M., and Shell, K. 1971. *The Economic Theory of Price Indexes.* Cambridge, Mass.: MIT Press.

Freeman, R.B. 1974. Overinvestment in College Education?. Mimeo., Harvard University.

——— 1976. *The Overeducated American.* New York: Academic Press.

——— 1977. The Decline in the Economic Rewards to College Education. *Review of Economics and Statistics* 54: 18–29.

—— 1978. Demographic Changes and the Age-Earnings Profile in the U.S., Discussion Paper 643, August. Institute of Economic Research, Harvard University.

Gollop, F.M. 1974. An Imperfect Product and Labor Markets Model: An Econometric Study, unpublished Ph.D. dissertation, Harvard University.

Gollop, F.M., and Jorgenson, D.W. 1980. U.S. Productivity Growth by Industry 1947–73. *New Developments in Productivity Measurements*, J.W. Kenrick and B. Vaccara, eds. New York: National Bureau of Economic Research.

Green, G.G. 1969. Comparing Employment Estimates for Household and Payroll Surveys. *Monthly Labor Review* 92: 9–14.

Griliches, Z. 1969. Capital-Skill Complementarity. *Review of Economics and Statistics* 51: 465–468.

—— 1970. Notes on the Role of Education in Production Functions and Growth Accounting. *Education, Income and Human Capital*, W.L. Hansen, ed. New York: National Bureau of Economic Research, pp. 70–119.

—— 1971. Hedonic Price Indexes Revisited. *Price Indexes and Quality Change*, Z. Griliches, ed. Cambridge, Mass.: Harvard University Press.

—— 1977. Estimating the Returns to Schooling: Some Econometric Problems. *Econometrica* 45: 1–22.

Gronau, R. 1974. Wage Comparisons—A Selectivity Bias. *Journal of Political Economy* 82: 1119–1144.

Hall, R.E., and Jorgenson, D.W. 1971. Application of the Theory of Optimum Capital Accumulation, *Tax Incentives and Capital Spending*, G. Fromm, ed. Washington, D.C.: The Brookings Institution.

Hulten, C.R. 1975. Technical Change and the Reproducibility of Capital. *American Economic Review* 65: 956–965.

Hulten, C.R., and Nishimizu, M. 1980. The Importance of Productivity Change in the Economic Growth of Nine Industrialized Countries. *Lagging Productivity Growth: Causes and Remedies*, Maital, S. and N. Meltz, eds. Cambridge, Mass.

Jorgenson, D.W., and Griliches, Z. 1967. The Explanation of Productivity Change. *Review of Economic Studies* 34: 249–283.

—— 1972. Issues in Growth Accounting: A Reply to E.F. Denison. *Survey of Current Business* 52: 65–94.

Kaun, D. 1965. Minimum Wages, Factor Substitution and Marginal Product. *Quarterly Journal of Economics* 79: 478–486.

Kendrick, J.W. 1973. *Postwar Productivity Trends in the United States*. New York: National Bureau of Economic Research.

Kuznets, S.S. 1971. *Modern Economic Growth.* New Haven: Yale University Press.

Lancaster, K. 1966. A New Approach to Consumer Theory. *Journal of Political Economy* 74: 132–156.

Lau, L.J. 1974. The Econometrics of Monotonicity, Convexity and Quasiconvexity, Discussion Paper, Institute for Mathematical Studies in the Social Sciences, Stanford University.

—— 1979. On Exact Index Numbers. *Review of Economics and Statistics* 61: 73–82.

Medoff, J. 1978. Substitution Between Workers with Different Demographic Characteristics in U.S. Manufacturing. mimeo., Harvard University.

Mitchell, E.J. 1969. Explaining the International Pattern of Labor Productivity and Wages: A Production Model with Two Labor Inputs. *Review of Economics and Statistics* 50: 461–469.

Moore, T.G. 1971. The Effect of Minimum Wages on Teenage Unemployment. *Journal of Political Economy* 79: 897–902.

Nelson, R.R. 1973. Recent Exercises in Growth Accounting: New Understanding or Dead End?, *American Economic Review* 63: 462–468.

Nelson, R.R., and Phelps, E.S. 1966. Investment in Humans, Technological Diffusion and Economic Growth. *American Economic Review* 56: 69–75.

Nordhaus, W. 1972. The Recent Productivity Slowdown. *Brookings Papers on Economic Activity* 3: 493–545.

Okner, B. 1972. Constructing a New Data Base from Existing Microdata Sets: The 1966 Merge File. *Annals of Social and Economic Measurement* 1: 325–342.

Psacharopoulos, G., and Hinchliffe, K. 1972. Further Evidence on the Elasticity of Substitution Among Different Types of Educated Labor. *Journal of Political Economy* 80: 786–792.

Rao, C.R. 1973. *Linear Statistical Inference and Its Applications.* New York: John Wiley.

Richter, M.K. 1966. Invariance Axioms and Economic Indexes. *Econometrica* 34: 739–755.

Rosen, S. 1969. On the Interindustry Wage and Hours Structure. *Journal of Political Economy* 77: 249–273.

—— 1974. Hedonic Prices and Implicit Markets: Product Differentiation in Pure Competition. *Journal of Political Economy* 82: 34–55.

Samuelson, P.A., and Swamy, S. 1974. Invariant Economic Index Numbers and Canonical Duality: Survey and Synthesis. *American Economic Review* 64: 566–593.

Sato, K. 1967. A Two-Level Constant Elasticity of Substitution Production Function. *Review of Economic Studies* 34: 201–218.

Schultz, T.W. 1971. *Investment in Human Capital*. New York: Free Press.

Solow, R.M. 1957. Technical Change and the Aggregate Production Function. *Review of Economics and Statistics* 39: 312–320.

Star, S. 1974. Accounting for the Growth of Output. *American Economic Review* 64: 123–135.

Star, S., and Hall, R.E. 1976. An Approximate Divisia Index of Total Factor Productivity. *Econometrica* 44: 257–264.

Theil, H. 1967. *Economics and Information Theory*. Amsterdam, North Holland: American Elsevier.

—— 1973. A New Index Number Formula. *Review of Economics and Statistics* 55: 498–502.

Tinbergen, J. 1975. *Income Distribution*. Amsterdam, North Holland: American Elsevier.

U. S. Department of Labor, Bureau of Labor Statistics. *Current Population Survey*. Washington, D.C.: Bureau of Labor Statistics, various issues.

——. *Special Labor Force Reports*. Washington, D.C.: Bureau of Labor Statistics, various issues.

U. S. Department of Commerce, Bureau of Economic Analysis. *Survey of Current Business*. Washington D.C.: Bureau of Economic Analysis, various issues.

——. *National Income and Product Accounts of the United States*, 1929–1965. Washington, D.C.: Bureau of Economic Analysis.

Vartia, Y.O. 1976. Ideal Log Change Index Numbers. *Scandinavian Journal of Statistics* 3: 121–126.

Waldorf, W. 1973. Quality of Labor in Manufacturing. *Review of Economics and Statistics* 55: 284–291.

Welch, F. 1969. Linear Synthesis of Skill Distributions. *Journal of Human Resources* 4: 311–327.

—— 1970. Education in Production. *Journal of Political Economy* 78: 35–59.

# INDEX